How to Make Money With Your Writer's Blog 101

The Basics
By E.T. Barton

By E.T. Barton

<u>Other Products by E.T. Barton:</u>

<u>HOW TO MAKE MONEY WITH YOUR WRITER'S BLOG 101 – THE BASICS</u>

<u>HOW TO MAKE MONEY WITH YOUR WRITER'S BLOG 202 – THE ADVANCED CLASS</u>

<u>THE ONE HOUR BOOKKEEPING METHOD</u>:

How To Do Your Books In One Hour Or Less

<u>HOW TO START A LUCRATIVE</u>

<u>VIRTUAL BOOKKEEPING BUSINESS</u>:

A Step-by-Step Guide to Working Less and Making More in the Bookkeeping Industry

<u>By E.T. Barton</u>

HOW TO DO A YEAR'S WORTH

OF BOOKKEEPING IN ONE DAY

A Step-by-Step Guide for Small Businesses

10 WAYS TO SAVE MONEY ON

BOOKKEEPING & ACCOUNTING

DIARY OF A BAD, BAD BOOKKEEPER

A Cautionary Embezzlement Tale

for Small Business Owners Everywhere

By E.T. Barton

Table of Contents

By E.T. Barton

~ v ~

By E.T. Barton

By E.T. Barton

By E.T. Barton

By E.T. Barton

INTRODUCTION

Welcome to "How to Make Money With Your Writer's Blog 101 – The Basics." This is a "Workshop" workbook created specifically for writer's who are struggling to make money with their independent writer's blog. I created this book during my very first workshop at my own writers group. It is a compilation of my experience as a blogger, advice I've gleaned from the Blogging Gurus (like Darren Rowse, Yaro Starok and Joel Comm), and advice I've learned from multiple writers workshops, conferences, eBooks, videos,

By E.T. Barton

marketing materials, etc. (I fully admit it...I am a Media Lush. I love all media forms that share knowledge, and I tend to test everything I learn. If something works, I pass it on. That means, *the information in this book will work.* I know it will because everything here has worked for me with my own blog.)

Here's what you're going to find in this book:

- 18 Lesson Plans: Since this book started as an online workshop where I was to post a lesson a day, I ended up with 18 individual plans that taught some aspect of blogging and making money blogging.
- 18 Assignments (each with sub-assignments): Okay, so technically, that's more than 18 assignments, but I don't feel like going through and counting them all, so I'm rounding down. Feel free to experiment or leave them as is.
- A Unique Opportunity to make $50 in this book. (I kid you not. I regularly pay my workshop

By E.T. Barton

attendees back MORE money than they paid for the workshop.)

- Blogging Basics

- A list of Plug-Ins that will make your website market itself in both the Search Engines and on your Social Media sites (i.e. Facebook, Twitter, LinkedIn, etc.)

- Website Links: If you are reading this in an eBook format, then all of the links should be active. When you click on them, you will be taken directly to the site where you can find more information on the corresponding items.

- Special Discount Links: Some of the companies in this book I am affiliated with. I became affiliated them only because I knew what they had to offer was an excellent and worthwhile deal. (I would never recommend something that I did not fully believe in.) Since I am affiliated with some of the sites, I was able to get "Special Discount Links" to some of the products, or special "Bonus" links. For example, JustHost

By E.T. Barton

offers a ton of free marketing credit on sites like Google Adwords, Facebook Ads and Yahoo!, to the people who are referred by subscribers or affiliates. And Google Adwords offers $75 of marketing credit to new marketers, but only to those who can find the coupon. (I found the coupon and linked to it in this book.)

- Multiple ways to make money on your website, both by selling your book and selling others.
- Other ways to make money with your blog 24/7, including Affiliate Income and selling Digital Products.
- And multiple ways to Automate your website and subscription list so you can do less work marketing and more work writing.

What more could a Money-Making Writer want?

And if you think this is good stuff, wait until you read *"How to Make Money with Your Writer's Blog 202 – The Advanced Class."* That book is where the REAL

By E.T. Barton

money will come in, as well as marketing advice that will take your book sales to the next level.

Also coming soon, *"Internet Marketing on a Dime: Mass Book Promotion for Minimum Cost"*.

By E.T. Barton

LESSON # 1: You Have to Spend Money to Make Money

Wait! Don't run away! Come back! I was only kidding.

Okay, I wasn't kidding...but now that I got you to open the first lesson, let me ask you a serious question:

Would you rather spend nothing to make $50, or would you rather spend $50 to make thousands? Because the answer to that question is going to dictate whether you make any money blogging or not.

You see, the one mistake a lot of bloggers make right out the gate (which will keep them from making money any decent kind of blogging dollars) is to choose a free blogging format. (Now let me explain my reasoning before you ditch this lesson and demand your money back.)

Here's my reasoning...

Why you shouldn't use a free blogging format:

1. When you use a free blogging format, **your money making options are instantly limited**. At Wordpress, you are not allowed to create any types of advertisements on your blog, or sell any types of products. At Blogger, the only ads you are allowed to place on your blog are Google Adsense ads (largely because Google owns Blogger.com). That means with the free Wordpress blog, you'll make NO money, and with the free Blogger blog, you'll make about $50 a year (if you're lucky). Right off the bat, that's a bad sign for a writer who is going to want to sell their books later on.

By E.T. Barton

2. Another reason a free blogging format isn't good is the fact that **the Plug-In options are limited**. Plug-Ins are like digital assistants that do tons of work for your 24/7, and all you have to do is set them up. The free blogging formats only allow certain Plug-Ins on your blog. Since Plug-Ins can do anything from sharing your blogs to hundreds and thousands of readers, to tracking which of your articles are the most popular, to creating ads for your books, you can see why you would want access to the best Plug-Ins available. In the long run, you will spend two to three times more of your time promoting your free blog than you would need to spend on a blog you pay for.

3. The third reason you should avoid the free blogging formats is because **when you choose the free blog, your background options are limited**. You have a very small selection of colors and menu bars, and while you can change some of the pictures in the

By E.T. Barton

template, your blog is still going to look like a million other free blogs out there. Only the paid option will allow you to set yourself apart from the pack and choose from hundreds of thousands of background themes – many many many of them free.

4. Finally, the fourth reason you should avoid a free blog is that **when you have one, you are stuck with the name of the blogging platform company in your domain name**. (For example, a free blog site for my own name would probably be ETBarton.Wordpress.com.) While there are ways around this, having the Blogging Platform name in your blog's name makes it harder for your fans to remember which site you're at (*"Was it Wordpress / Blogger / Freeforum...?"*), as well as harder for them to share your articles with their friends and family. So, make it easy for them (and yourself) from the beginning by ditching the extra word in the domain. Your motive

should always be, "Easy for my readers to find."

Now that you have an idea of why you should choose a paid blog over a free blog, let's do a price tally to give you an idea of what you're actually paying for.

THE COST:

For around $50 A YEAR, you can buy a domain name and pay for a year's worth of hosting. Once you have the site available, you instantly get FREE access to thousands of Plug-Ins and thousands of Backgrounds. On top of that, many hosting companies will allow you to host UNLIMITED ADDITIONAL domain names for that low $4.45/ month price – you just have to pay for the domain name, which will cost you about $15 each. (Again, the first domain name is included in the $50 Hosting Price.)

OPTIONAL:

By E.T. Barton

You can pay a third party site to submit your blog to all of the search engine sites, but that is completely optional since you can also do the work for yourself. Eventually, you will want to pay to have someone to host your email list, but we'll get into that later.

RECOMMENDED HOSTING COMPANY:

While there are many hosting sites out there that will host your site, I like JustHost.com. This is where I host my many *many* blogs for $50 a year. I like them because you buy the domain name at the company, click on their Wordpress button, type in the name and login information you want, and within 20 minutes, they've set up a basic PAID Wordpress account for you. You can then go to Wordpress, login with the information you chose, and start customizing that site. Not only is JustHost easy, but it's cheap. What could be better?

Click on this link here and you can get the following Free Ad Credits just for Joining at sites like Google, Facebook, Yahoo and MySpace:

(If the link doesn't work for you, type in this info to get your free credit:

http://stats.justhost.com/track?c07deccfba093215642933 6cc8836667d)

WHAT IF I ALREADY HAVE A FREE BLOG?

Take heart...even if you've had a free blog for a long time, you can easily "Export" a backup of your entire current blog and "Import" it into a paid blog. It takes only a few minutes, and all of your blogs and comments will be imported right along with the transfer. (If you need help with that, email me at Erica@ETBarton.net and I will send you instructions.)

By E.T. Barton

WORDPRESS VERSUS BLOGGER

While there are tons of free blogging sites you could go with to host your site, in the blogging world, all of the experts agree that bloggers should go with one of the top two – Wordpress or Blogger. As I stated earlier, Blogger is owned by Google, which can be beneficial when you utilize the Google services to promote your blog and make money. Blogger is a very basic program that makes it easy for a lot of newbies to use.

Having said that, the *"Big-Money-Making Bloggers"* I listen to all agree that Wordpress is the best. More people throw their development time into Wordpress themes and Plug-Ins instead of Blogger, which makes Wordpress the IPad of the blogging industry. While I admit that I do use Wordpress and most of my knowledge and advice will be a bit more tailored toward Wordpress because of it, I will not presume to tell you which blogging platform you absolutely must use. (Wordpress rocks! ☺)

WARNING: DO NOT SIGN UP FOR A WORDPRESS OR BLOGGER BLOG TONIGHT IF YOU DON'T HAVE ONE ALREADY. INSTEAD, WAIT UNTIL YOU'VE READ A FEW MORE LESSONS. I say this because once you read some of the upcoming lessons, you may want to change your domain name or switch hosting companies. In many cases, it will be easier to set up your new blog with your new hosting company, so for now, DON'T sign up for a paid account if you don't already have one.

YOUR ASSIGNMENT (should you wish to accept it):

For tonight, if you aren't with Wordpress or Blogger, or if you don't have a paid website, go ahead and check out the two main blogging programs and see which one appeals to you most. You may also want to Google "Free Wordpress / Blogger Themes for (whatever topic you blog about)." That way, you can get an idea of what you might want your blog to look like, and which platform will offer you the look that appeals to you most.

How to Make Money With Your Writers Blog 101: The Basics

By E.T. Barton

LESSON # 2: Domain Name Do's and Don'ts

Now that I've given you some thoughts on free blogs versus paid blogs, let's talk about domain names. Too often, people choose domain names that are confusing and hard to remember. While you should definitely use your writer's pen name as a domain name for your writer's website, your name alone may not be enough to drive traffic to that website. A blog – especially a "niche" blog – will go farther in attracting traffic from search engines than a name alone would be. By blogging on a niche blog, you can set yourself apart as an expert, which can help drive traffic to your writer's

By E.T. Barton

blog as people get to know you. (In other words, start thinking in terms of having multiple blogs to promote your writer's blog.)

Let me state this another way. If you blog under your name, people won't know what you're blogging about unless they read the body of your work. If you blog on a niche blog (or SEVERAL niche blogs), you have the opportunity to build your name brand as an expert in multiple fields, and people will begin seeking you out for answers. Then, once they get to know you, they will buy your books just because they love what you have to say.

As an example, Suzanne Lazear from LARA blogs on a Steampunk blog. She also spoke at the last conference on a Steampunk topic, which was a very successful workshop. She is building her brand as a Steampunk expert, and people who love Steampunk will run out and buy her book the moment it hits the shelves. That's the kind of reputation we should all be building when focusing on blogging.

(And by the way, when I say "website", I mean a site that only changes occasionally versus a blog which changes constantly.)

Tomorrow, I will discuss keywords and how they can drive traffic to your site from the search engines, so wait until then before you run out and buy any new domain names. In the meantime, here are some dos and don'ts when choosing a domain name:

1. **Don't Use Complicated Words or Names:** Do yourself a favor...when you pick the name of a website...go with something simple. If your first or last name is hard to remember or confusing (and you know if it is), then don't use it in the website link. You want people to be able to find you and to remember your blog's name without going "How was that spelled again?" So something like... "*Supercalifragilisticexpialidocious*.com" would be bad, even if you spelled it "*Super-Cali-Fragilistic-Expi-Ali-Docious*.com." Instead, shorten it and try "SuperBlogger.com", or go

with the name of your niche or genre – as long as it's simple, easy to remember and easy to spell.

2. **Don't Make The Website Name Too Long** – as also shown in the example above, keep it short. A long name doesn't fit nicely in any kind of communication, whether Word documents, letterhead, or even on bookmarks. Short is quick and easy to type...and that's the goal.

3. **Don't Make it "Forgettable**." We've all done it. We've all forgotten someone's exact website address and ended up at the wrong site. We assume a website name should be obvious, but it instead ends up being complicated. For example, "American Airlines" is NOT at AmericanAirlines.com. Instead, they are at AA.COM. And AA (i.e. Alcoholics Anonymous) is at AA.ORG. And then of course, there's the Auto Club, which is not at AutoClub.com, but is at AAA.com instead. That's not confusing, right? Personally, I forget American Airlines' website every time I want to go to them. I have to Google the site each time

to make sure I end up at the right website. The end result? I fly United instead. Their website's easier to find...United.com. Therefore, name your website something associated to your brand or genre, and name it something your readers can remember.

4. **Don't Use "Characters."** Putting "&," "-"or "_" signs in your website name is a HUGE pain-in-the-keester for your readers to type. It slows your reader down, and you don't want to slow them down when they come to your site. It's also easy to forget the characters, so they may not end up at your site at all. On the other hand, typing "and" or leaving out the dashes is much easier and faster for someone to type. So, be super easy, and super convenient in everything you do – including naming your website.

5. **Don't Use Numbers** – unless of course the numbers are part of your business name. For example, 123Inkjets.com is a great Business Name (and thus website name by association) because 1) the 123 is easy to remember, and 2)

the numbers at the beginning of the word pretty much guarantee the website first billing in any Phone Book or Internet Directory they list themselves in. Any number sequence that's really easy to remember can help move your site up in a local directory, BUT on the flip side, picking a website like SuperBlogger**99**.com is not a good idea. Even though the 99 may be memorable, people are still going to ask you, *"Why 99?"* If your answer is, *"Because SuperBlogger.com was already taken and the name generator suggested the 99"*...well guess what...you've lost your reader's attention at the words, "already taken." And when they go to search your website, they're going to forget the "99" part in your website url. Instead, they'll end up at the original SuperBlogger.com website – your competition – and they'll forget all about you.

a. **Other Examples of good numbers:** 123, 321, 1800 (*as in 1-800*), 50, 100,

101, 1001. Basically, anything ending in 1,5, or 0 is usually easier to remember.

b. **Examples of bad numbers:** There was a great website I went to once. It was called 46things.com – or was it 47? Or 48? Or maybe it was 30 something. Whatever it was, I LOVED the website, and I found it because it was suggested by a book I read. But guess what – I never found the website again. I couldn't remember the name, and even when I tried Googling it, nothing came up. The idea and concept behind the website was fantastic, but because the number was not easy to remember, they lost me as a reader. And if they lost me – they've probably lost many other people as well. After all, I'm just an Average American Girl. (Other numbers to forget about – 1866, 1877, 1888, and anything *not* ending in 1,5, or 0. They're harder to remember.)

~ 22 ~

6. **Oh yeah – and DEFINITELY ditch the ".wordpress" or ".blogger" in your domain name.** Again, it makes it hard for readers to remember which site you're at.

   a. If you already own a site with "wordpress," "blogger" or some other blogging name in it, and you don't want to get a new paid website, then buy the domain name for your site (it can cost as little as $10 a year). Once you own the domain name, you can do a "Forward" or a "Masked Forward" with the company you buy the Domain name from. What that means is that anyone could then type in the name of your domain name (i.e. MyName.com) and they would be redirected to your blog site with the "wordpress" or "blogger" name in the url. With a Forward, the name they typed will disappear and show the name with the wordpress/blogger name in it. With a Masked Forward, the domain name will remain, hiding the wordpress or blogger part. Your visitor will never know they are at a free blogging site, and they won't have to remember which site when they come visit you.

b. A Few Recommended Domain Sites and Prices: Again, if you are only going to get a domain name and forward it, there are a couple sites I recommend.

   i. JustHost.com is my favorite and they charge only $15 per domain name. If you go with them to buy a domain name and then decide to create a website around that domain name, you won't have to pay anything to transfer your domain name over from another site. (They usually charge $50 to help you transfer your site.)

   ii. GoDaddy.com usually costs $12 a year for a domain name, or $2 for the Domain name IF you host with them for $4.49 a year. Click here if you want to get a special hosting discount of $1.99 a month for the first three months, or type in: http://www.anrdoezrs.net/click-3990205-10378494. This is the special deal link I was able to find with them.

iii. Yahoo.com costs $12 a month to host with the site, but only $10 to buy a Domain name. If you simply want to own a domain name and then forward it, I LOVE Yahoo! because it can all be handled within your Yahoo! email. In fact, Yahoo! will even create an easy-to-access email link to your website domain, so you don't have to create a website to have people write to you at something like emailme@myname.com. They also have an easy sitebuilder if you want to set up a single page for your domain name, or a more complex website later on. But again, hosting is expensive at $12 a month, and if you want to transfer it to a new hosting company, it will cost at least $50 to do that. Either way, here is a "special deal" link that will get you 25% off your hosting fees: http://www.jdoqocy.com/click-2775681-10556305

Okay – I've given you a list of what NOT to do when naming your domain name. If you have any of these "don'ts" in your domain name, start thinking about what domain name might be easier to find. Also, if you only have a blog in your writer's name, KEEP IT, but consider starting a "Niche" blog (or two) that focuses on a topic you love in addition to your website. Your website will be your bookstore, while your blog will make people fall in love with your writing style. (I will touch more on these subjects later in the week.)

YOUR ASSIGNMENT (should you wish to accept it):

If you're thinking of starting a blog or changing your blog name, start Googling some ideas to see what's out there, and who has the name you want. BUT...DO NOT BUY ANY DOMAIN NAMES YET!!! The Keyword Lesson coming up is very important for driving traffic, and you can actually use a keyword phrase as a domain name. So... feel free to surf, but do NOT buy anything, and do not spend too much time on this. By the end of the workshop, you WILL be tired of the internet. Save your energy.

By E.T. Barton

LESSON # 3: The Importance of Keywords

(Quick Note: Keywords can be very confusing...so you will probably want to read this lesson twice.   Read it through once to get a basic understanding, then read it again for the content.)

For now, I am going to drone on for quite a while about keywords. The reason for this is because they are *so very important* when it comes to blogs and websites. **Keywords give you free advertising.**   They tell the Google Spiders (and other Search Engine robots) – as well as all your visitors – exactly what your site is about. You can use them in your titles, your catch phrases, your articles, your meta tags, and even your domain name.

Keywords can create a brand for you that search engines love and people remember.

Here's an example of keywords on a strong website:

Have you ever "Googled" the expression "Romance Writers", and then received 10 million website results?   "Romance Writers" is a keyword phrase. The first result that's probably going to pop up is "Romance Writers of America."   RWA gets the # 1 position in the Google Search Engine because 1) they get so many hits every month (from 10,000+ members plus all the people looking to become romance writers), and 2) their website is filled with tons of Keywords and Keyword Phrases. Take a look:

By E.T. Barton

Right at the top, where they're tagline belongs, you see the words "<u>Romance Writers</u> of America." Other strong keyword phrases include "<u>RWA</u>" (Romance Writers of America's brand), "<u>The Romance Genre</u>", "<u>Booksellers & Librarians</u>" and even "<u>RITA & Golden Heart</u>." Next, you see their "About Info" in the main section of this page, with the keyword phrase, "The Voice of <u>Romance Fiction</u>." Anyone looking for any of these keyword phrases will be directed to this website because this page is loaded with similar keywords and because *they already get so much traffic.*

In a similar fashion, the more you dominate in your niche / genre because of your keywords and traffic,

By E.T. Barton

the higher your blog will be pushed in the Search Engine Lists. The higher you are in the Search Engine Lists, the more free (i.e. "Organic") traffic will be sent to your blog. (To put it another way – think of the NYT Bestseller list. If you make it onto that list, tons of people will rush out and buy your book. The only way to get on that Bestseller list is to sell a ton of a books in a very short period of time. Search Engines are the same way. To dominate them, you need a LOT of traffic in a very short time. When you get it, then they will send you more.)

Okay, so I've told you why Keywords and Keyword Phrases are important. Now let's talk about where you can use them, and how to find out the keywords your readers are searching for (so you can drive your blog up in the Search Engines and dominate your niche).

Real Quick "Must-Know" Definitions:

A Catch Phrase is exactly what it sounds like...a Phrase that "Catches" someone's attention. It's usually catchy and sticks in your head like the song, "It's a Small World." It's hard to forget – or tune out even when you *really want to* – and you can fit it on a business card.

A Tagline is a sentence on a blog (or website) that tells visitors what that site is all about. It also tells search engines, like Google, what that site is about so they can recommend your site to people looking for you and your products. (i.e. It is free marketing).

A Keyword is a word or phrase that people use to search for *anything* from products to advice and even "How to write romance." People use keywords when they want answers to problems...like "What is Bookkeeping?" or even to find the "New York Times Bestselling List." They would Google those expressions to find definitions or products, and if keywords on your blog match those searches, you have a better chance of having those Search Engines send seekers to your blog.

By E.T. Barton

Even though the definitions for Catch Phrase, Tagline and Keyword are different, *these three things don't have to be*. In fact, I recommend that you make these three things the SAME in order to Brand you and your business into the minds of every blog visitor and potential customer you get. Figure out a catch phrase that's small enough to fit on a business card, but filled with tagline keywords that will also tell your reader what your blog (and your company) is about. Put it all together into one sentence and you will create a catch phrase that people will remember. Then, put that catch phrase on your blog where your tagline belongs (right at the top, under the title of your blog), on your website, on your business cards, magnetic signs, brochures...*everything*. Once you do, you will create one of the most powerful marketing tools available to help you sell your products and attract people to your business.

By E.T. Barton

Tagline Checklist

When you come up with a tagline for the top of your blog, you need to make sure your tagline tells your visitors what your blog (and your business) is about. To do this effectively, you need to focus on stringing together powerful Keywords into something clever, and hopefully related to your blog's domain name. By doing so, you increase your position in the Search Engines automatically. You may not make it to # 1 for a while (after all, you are competing with other blogs that have had more blog posts, hits, readers, and visitors), but it definitely gives your site a fighting chance.

Why You Want Keywords in Your Tagline

I'm sure many of you already have your tagline in mind. You probably use it already in your email signature line and on your business cards. You're probably already booting up your blog and typing it into your website...but STOP!... I'm probably going to blow your tagline right out of the water in the next subsection.

More than likely, you're going to have to <u>forget about using your current catch phrase on your blog</u>, and <u>only use it on your website</u>. Since your blog is going to be your main traffic magnet, you want very powerful keywords in your tagline because... (*now pay attention here*)... <u>every time you post a blog, and every time you create a page on your blog, that tagline is going to be the first thing the search engine spiders see...again, and again, and again.</u> It's going to repeat every time you create something new on your site (without any extra work from you), and the spiders will find it every single time. Soon, you'll be the go-to site for whatever keyword phrase you chose in your tagline.

Okay – let's move on to making you hate me. ☺

Finding Powerful Keywords

So you know you want keywords on your website, and you know you want them in your tagline, blog posts, your "About" page, and possibly IN your domain name. But you want powerful keywords, right? You want the keywords no one else is using, but that all your readers are searching for. Where do you start? How do you know what keywords your readers are looking for, and what keywords are the most popular? And your competition – the other bloggers in your niche – how do you know if they are using those same keywords?

I'm so glad you asked...you're brilliant for thinking of these things. ☺

There are AT LEAST THREE places that will tell you EXACTLY how many people are "Googling" certain keyword phrases, how often they're using other search engines, and how many of your competitors are using those same keywords. Those sites are Google Adwords, Wordtracker.com, or Wordze.com. When you go to those sites, you can type in the name of your niche, and immediately get thousands of suggestions on keyword phrases that your readers are using. Not only will this information help you create a powerful tagline, but it can also help you write articles that specifically answer your readers' questions. In other words, it will tell you what your readers want. All you have to do is type in an expression, hit "Search" or "Go" and BAM!, there it is, in a format you can download, save, and use for a long time.

Again, to find Keywords that you can add to your website's tagline – and your website in general – check out Google Adwords, Wordtracker.com, or Wordze.com. All three offer search results for various keywords, as well as competition for those keywords, and related search terms.

Another good site to check out and see what competing blogs are using is to go to www.Compete.com. That site will actually tell you what keywords your competitors pay for to bring visitors, as well as the Organic Keywords they use to get free traffic.

Finally, a tool I discovered recently that works really well is Keyword Winner. It is a Plug-In that you install in your Wordpress account. Then, whenever you open up a New Post page, you will see the Keyword Winner recommendation box right beneath your Title Box. You can then type in the topic or theme of your

By E.T. Barton

blog post and click "Get Suggestions." When you do, the Keyword Winner will come back with stats about how much competition you will have for that phrase in the past month, as well as the number of competitive sites have used that expression, and the number of times people "Googled" that keyword phrase. It will also suggest alternative keyword phrases with lower competition numbers and scores. If you take a keyword phrase with the lowest score and competition, you will dominate that keyword expression and increase the traffic from the Search Engine Spiders. (The tool is $47 for one blog site, which is high, but you only pay for it once and you own it forever. Wordze and Wordtracker on the other hand, have a monthly fee of around $40. So compared to a monthly fee, this is a good and convenient product to get.")

An Example from a Past Class – Kathy:

Kathy is a writer who blogs about her "day job" as a police woman. She had a fantastic catch phrase on her blog: "Authentic Crime...Arresting Stories". This is definitely a catch phrase to put on her writer's WEBSITE (not blog) as a tagline, as well as any business cards, buttons, etc. It's memorable, clever, funny, and it tells her visitors what kind of stories she writes...memorable, clever, and funny cop stories.

Unfortunately, when I put "Authentic Crime" and "Arresting Stories" into Wordtracker, I find that no one is Googling those keyword phrases. Why would they? Kathy hasn't made that expression famous yet. Once she has become famous, and her blog and website are kicking butt, then the phrase will become popular and people might use it to see who first came up with the phrase, or to find Kathy herself. But until that day, that catch phrase is bringing her NO TRAFFIC, and so it's better left on the back burner (which again, is business cards, a website, bookmarks, etc.).

But I'm not done with Kathy...not by a long shot.

You'll notice I said that Kathy writes "memorable, clever, and funny cop stories." The term "cop stories" is the subject of that sentence, which makes it an ideal niche for her blog, and a keyword phrase to

By E.T. Barton

search for. If Kathy chose to write about being a cop on her blog, or any kind of information relating to being a cop, and if she chose the right keywords, she could easily dominate the niche about cop stories very quickly, which could potentially skyrocket her book sales later on (book sales being her business). Take a look at the top results for "Cop Stories" as a keyword. (This is from Wordtracker.)

Keyword (?) (15)	Searches (?) (19)	In Anchor And Title (?)	KEI (?)	KEI3 (?)	Google Count ▼ (?)	Google Count (quoted) (?)
1 ☑ cop stories (search)	1	207	0.000	0.005	18,000,000 ↵	23,100 ↵
2 ☑ cop stones (search)	1	–	–	–	18,000,000 ↵	23,100 ↵
3 ☑ funny cop stories (search)	4	7	0.356	0.571	3,370,000 ↵	69,200 ↵
4 ☑ quarter cop bra stories (search)	1	1	0.333	1.00	2,280,000 ↵	2,210 ↵
5 ☑ long fingernails gouge cop stories (search)	1	0	–	–	2,110,000 ↵	0 ↵
6 ☑ grand theft auto vice city stories cop cheat for psp (search)	1	0	–	–	1,050,000 ↵	0 ↵
7 ☑ bad cop stories (search)	1	–	–	–	379,000 ↵	1,210,000 ↵
8 ☑ animal cop stories (search)	1	0	–	–	298,000 ↵	6 ↵
9 ☑ grand theft auto vice city stories cop cheat (search)	1	0	–	–	160,000 ↵	0 ↵
10 ☑ januarys corrupt cop stories (search)	1	0	–	–	140,000 ↵	0 ↵
11 ☑ dumb cop stories (search)	2	1	1.00	2.00	120,000 ↵	71 ↵

Get additional metrics ➜ Export: Keywords only or all columns

Select: Select keywords containing: Delete selected: Save Selected:

All None   [Select] [Deselect]   [Delete]   [Save]

~ 41 ~

First, I put in "Cop Stories" and then I asked Wordtracker to "Get Additional Metrics" (the purple link in the top left corner of the picture). By doing so, I was able to get Wordtracker's analysis, as well as the Google Counts, which are more important because Google dominates the Search Engines at this point in time.

Next, I clicked on Google Count so that I could put them in order by the number of times the Keyword to the right was searched. As you can see, "Cop Stories" was searched approximately 18 million times. (Unfortunately, Google won't tell you if that's per month or per year, but as you can deduce, that's a lot of searching for "Cop Stories.")

Now check out the "In Anchor and Title" column (i.e., the Tagline). Wordtracker says they've found 207 websites with the Keyword Phrase "Cop Stories" in their Tagline or domain name. Interesting...

Finally, to the far right, you will see the "Google Count (Quoted)." That number is the total number of websites/blogs/posts that Google's spiders have associated with that Keyword Phrase.

When you put all these statistics together, you can see that 18 million people are searching for "Cop Stories" and only 23,100 websites are answering that specific need. That means, "Cop Stories" would be a Powerful Keyword Phrase to use in her tagline, blog posts, domain name, meta tags, and even her titles. In fact, CopStories.com would be a great blog domain name, although someone has already parked it. If Kathy wanted that domain name, she would have to buy it for a fairly hefty sum of money. So instead, she may want to just use the expression in her tagline, and keep looking for a different domain name.

Hold on though...check out # 5 on the list. More than 2 million people are searching the phrase "long fingernails gouge cop stories" and yet there are NO websites catering to that. Now, I'm not suggesting that Kathy start a blog about long fingernails gouging cops, BUT...that might be an interesting twist in one of her books. ☺ Even if she NEVER uses that in her tagline, she could use that in a blog post, a title, and her meta tags (the keywords you use in your post to describe the post) and she could draw a lot of traffic to that one particular blog post, and thus her blog. From there, it's up to her to convert a one-time reader into a return reader.

Furthermore, she doesn't have to use "long fingernails gouge cop stories" verbatim. Often, you could add a few extra words to satisfy that search (For example, maybe a title like, "A Woman with <u>Long Fingernails Gouges</u> a <u>Cop</u> – <u>Stories</u> of Cops and the Crazy Women they Deal With") and Google will still recognize it as that keyword phrase people are searching for, and begin sending people to that article as Kathy's site moves up in the ranking.

Therefore, by using a tool like Wordtracker, you can create some very powerful domain names, taglines, blog posts, and so on very, very easily.

YOUR ASSIGNMENT:

1. **Go to** Wordtracker.com **and/or** Wordze.com **and sign up for their FREE trials.** You don't have to keep the subscription, but if you at least sign up for it, you can run as many keyword searches as you want from the websites, and then download the results into an Excel file that you can keep LONG AFTER you cancel the subscription. So start with Wordtracker and have fun for 7 days... then cancel it and check out Wordze for 30 days. Both will get you more free keywords and results than you'll ever know what to do with.

2. **Play around with some Keywords and see what kind of Tagline you can come up with.**

3. **Go to Adwords.Google.com and Play with their Keyword Tool.** (It's Free.) Use the following link to get an account and you will get $75 toward any future advertising campaign you want...at *no cost*:

https://services.google.com/fb/forms/adwordscou
pon/?site=u-adwords-
hp&utm_term=banner2u&utm_source=en-us-ha-
rm-adwords-
hp&utm_medium=ad&utm_campaign=en

4. **Once you have a Tagline, make sure to add it to your Blog. Also, don't forget – make sure the title of your blog is right ABOVE your tagline.** (To do this in Wordpress, log in, find your "Settings" link, and then click "General." You will see the Blog Title and the Tagline right at the top.

5. **While you are logged into your blog, change your "Permalink Settings" so that the name is included in the link to your articles.** Usually, when you create a blog post, your blogging platform will automate a link to that article. By changing your Permalink to include the "Name" of the title in the link, each blog post will automatically create an extra Keyword stamp in the URL that the Search Engine Spiders love.

By E.T. Barton

It's a very simple way to double your Keyword Impact without a lot of extra work.

6. **Finally, the next time you write a blog, try to slip some of the keywords you find into the blog post, especially the first paragraph.** Often, Search Engine Spiders only analyze the first paragraph before moving on. The more keywords you have in the first paragraph of the post, the more memorable that article will be to the Search Engine Spiders.

By E.T. Barton

LESSON # 4: Blogging Goals

So I've given you the very basest foundation for blogging on how to make money. The first point was to make sure you have a paid blog – because if you don't have one, you WON'T make any money with your writer's blog, PERIOD. The second lesson was about choosing domain names that will make it easy to find you. The third lesson was about using keywords on your blog, and especially in your domain name or tagline.

Next, we're going to talk about your future – or more precisely, the future of you and your blog. Tonight, we're going to set some goals for you to focus on as you build this blog. Hopefully, these goals will be a reminder of what you're working for every time you get frustrated, or feel a bit off track. Since this is a fairly important lesson (like all my lessons, of course), you're probably going to want to print the last page and post it somewhere (because the last page will be a recap of your goals).

But first...a random thought from you sponsor.

Why Should I Have a Blog? Who Really Cares?

During the 2010 Romance Writers of America conference, everywhere you went, you heard publishers saying two things: 1) a writer with fans (whether unpublished or published) was a valuable asset to a publishing house, and 2) a writer's email subscription list is "Gold" (especially to the Editors). Having fans means instant sales to publishers – sales they don't have to do because the writer has already done it for them. That right there was the best reason I heard for why people should be blogging – because it will make you more money right out the gate every time one of your books is published, and the more subscribers you have to your blog, the better chance you have of hitting the New York Times Bestselling List when your books come out. So be aggressive with your blog and when attracting traffic. Those readers are your ticket to the big times (even before you get published).

How Many Subscribers Do I Want Before I Can Start Relaxing?

I once heard a statistic from one of my blogging gurus – Yaro Starak - who regularly has six-figure launches of his blogging products. (Those products are usually videos or eBooks, but the logic is sound for regular books as well.) He said that if you to have a six-figure launch, you need to have at least 5,000 subscribers to your blog. Those subscribers can be through email or RSS, but it's really the email lists

By E.T. Barton

that your publisher (or future publisher) is going to want. The subscribers to your email list have already agreed to have you tell them about any products you endorse, they already have a relationship with you, and they will be more than thrilled to buy your own products as soon as they hit the shelves. So keep that goal in mind: You want 5,000 subscribers to your blog BEFORE your next book (or first book) comes out. Once you get that many subscribers, you can start relaxing. (And yes, I will teach about the email list and how to work on getting 5,000 subscribers later in the workshop.)

How Often Should You Post to Your Blog?

I know this is a question a lot of Bloggers wonder when blogging. "Should I blog once a week? Once a month? Only when I'm inspired?" Should I post a whole bunch of blogs at once, or save them for days when my mind's in a funk? And does it really matter WHEN I blog, as long as I do? What is the standard?" And for those of you who are really skeptical about this class (*this is where I lift a condescending eyebrow)...* "Isn't blogging 'occasionally' better than 'not blogging at all'? And in actuality, isn't all this advice just subjective conjecture anyway?"

What I am about to say may surprise you. (Then again, it may not.)

Believe it or not, there IS a standard you should live by when it comes to blogging. According to all of the Blogging Gurus (like Darren Rowse, Yaro Starak, Joel Comm, etc), to run a successful blog, you need to blog AT LEAST ONCE A WEEK.

I'll say it again: **If you want your blog to be successful, you need to blog at least once a week.**

Believe me, as a writer who also blogs, I know how difficult this can be. You have to work your regular jobs (whether it's writing or something else), spend time with your families and living your life, write the book of your heart, and then find time for THIS? Sheesh...it can make your head explode.

Take heart. It's not as difficult as you think.

For one thing – you don't have to blog alone. You CAN find someone to help you. In fact, here are several things you can do to fill the once a week slot (for when you're too tired to do it yourself). You could...

- Put out a call on your blog asking for guest bloggers and have THEIR blog be the blog of the week.
- Find free blog articles to share on your blog at tons of free article sites like EzineArticles.com.
- Pay someone to blog for you.
- Post "Other" types of media on your blog to fulfill this requirement (media like YouTube videos, podcasts, and interviews).
- Do surveys.
- Make announcements.
- Run contests.
- You could even run a "Carnival" of blogs where you share 3 to 5 links to blog articles you found interesting.

By E.T. Barton

Those are just a few to start. And since there is no law that says your blog has to be strictly YOU and YOUR VOICE, why not branch out? In fact, the more you branch out, the faster your blog will become popular. There are tons of ways to blog, even though not a lot of bloggers are doing it. (Not even THIS blogger.)

As to WHEN you should be blogging, I have an answer to that as well.

The other questions bloggers ask is: "Is it better to blog in the morning, at night, during the week, or on the weekends?" The answer to that is... sometime between Monday and Wednesday of each week. Here's why...

(*Later in the workshop, I am going to do an intensive lesson on Twitter – one of the most valuable tools a Blogger has in their arsenal. Just using Twitter alone can make your blog successful without any advertising at all, and it can help you get regular readers.   But again, that will come later in the workshop.*)

Since Twitter is one of the most important tools a Blogger has, it is an excellent idea to post your blog during Twitter's Peak Times. It is the general consensus among the blogging gurus that Twitter's Peak Times are between Monday and Wednesday during any week. Yes, Twitter still gets tons of hits at other times during the week, but it seems to be that most people jump on Twitter when they return to work on Monday, and continue to surf until Wednesday, the day that everything starts feeling like old news. Maybe it's because they have a computer at work and they are avoiding doing what they should be doing, or maybe it's because they're busy doing other things on the weekend, but most of the statistics you find about Twitter will agree; **traffic is highest on the first three days of the workweek and lowest on the weekends.**

Therefore, if you want to direct the highest amount of traffic to your blog, you should consider posting during Twitter's peak hours – Monday through Wednesday of each week.

You should also test to see when posting has the highest peaks on your website. For some, you may find that your traffic is higher in the morning than in the evening. For others, it might be night time. You won't know unless you use a Plug-In like "Clicky" or "Google Analytics," which will give you a lovely little graphics depicting your blog's peak traffic hits.So once again – to answer the question in the title about when you should be posting – **You should post at least once a week, between Monday and Wednesday of that week, in order to get the most traffic to your blog.** The exact time of day during those three days will depend entirely on your readers. You need to test post at different times of the day and night in order to see when you get the highest traffic spikes, and to know when the actual "best posting time for your blog" is.

ONE FINAL NOTE (before anyone emails me with the phrase, "But I am most creative during the hours of... on..."):

If you noticed, I said "You should <u>POST</u>" – NOT "write." In every blog I've seen, there is always an option to "Publish" a blog at a later time and date. If your peak writing times fall on a weekend, don't

By E.T. Barton

despair. Write as many blogs as you can during that peak period, and then "Post Date" your post for once a week, twice a week, a year later...whatever date you would like that posting to show up on your blog. That way, if you've written tons of blogs on a particular topic, you can set them up for posting all on that same day, and then not have to worry about your blog until next month. It's an easier way to blog for anyone who worries about their time constraints (which is all of us, right?).

YOUR ASSIGNMENT (should you wish to accept it):

1. **Find some Statistic Plug-Ins for your website and "Install", then "Activate" them:** I like KStats, Clicky, and Google Analytics for Wordpress. *If you have some you prefer – especially those of you who are on other Blogging platforms – please share them on the Loop.*

a. To Add Plug-ins on Wordpress, go to "Plug-ins", then "Add New", and then type in the names above. When you find them, click "Install" to the left, and then "Activate" when you see it...(it should look like this):

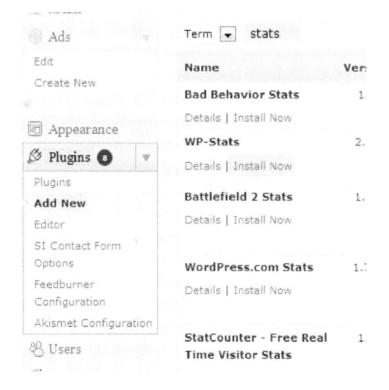

By E.T. Barton

2. **Write two blog posts for your blog and post one on Monday <u>Morning,</u> and postdate the second one for the following Monday <u>Afternoon.</u>** I don't care if they're generic posts – just post them. Then, check back and see which had a higher spike. While you probably won't see much difference now – be patient. You will start to see some differences later this month.

Your Goals Recapped:

<u>**You should post at least once a week, between Monday and Wednesday, in order to get the most traffic to your blog.**</u>

To Post Those Blogs, You Could...

- Put out a call on your blog asking for guest bloggers and have THEIR blog be the blog of the week.

- Find free blog articles to share on your blog at tons of free article sites.
- Pay someone to blog for you.
- Post "Other" types of media on your blog to fulfill this requirement (media like YouTube videos, podcasts, and interviews).
- Do surveys.
- Make announcements.
- Run contests.
- You could even run a "Carnival" of blogs where you share 3 to 5 links to blog articles you found interesting.

Finally, be aggressive in your marketing and blogging until you have 5,000 subscribers, AND try to get those 5,000 subscribers BEFORE you actually publish your next book.

Keep at it... you *will* get it done.

By E.T. Barton

LESSON # 5: Seven Ways to Get and Keep Your Readers' Attention

I once read an article that said Internet Surfers will stay on a website an average of NINE SECONDS before they move on. That's it – that's all you have... nine seconds to make an impression before you lose them for good. (This should not be a new concept to any of you since you are all writers and you should all know the "5-Page Hook" concept.) So the important question I'm going to answer tonight is: **How can YOU make**

By E.T. Barton

your readers stay longer (thus increasing your chances of turning them into subscribers)?

Here are the basic facts. The average internet reader has a shorter attention span than your average book reader. The usual reasons are that they're either 1) looking for something in particular and they're checking out your site from a search engine, or 2) they're just screwing around, killing time, and thus are looking for interesting and intriguing information. (Of course, there are many other reasons people surf the internet, but for now, let's just keep things simple and stick with those two reasons.) Keeping those two things in mind, you quickly realize that in nine seconds, a surfer will basically skim a blog post and make a decision on whether or not they like it based on the look of the blog post, and possibly the first paragraph. If they like it, they'll read more. If they don't, they'll bounce. You can keep them longer if you catch their eye and their interest. Doing that is very simple.

One more thing you want to keep in mind is this: <u>Internet Readers WANT to skim...they DON'T want to waste their time all day long on one blog</u>. If you focus on that concept – on making your blog "skimmable," you will suck them in and keep them longer than they planned. By delivering what they want, you give them a reason to look through your whole blog site and see what else you write. That's how you're going to suck them in, and that's how you're going to keep them. The following will show you how to make your Blog "Skimmable":

1. The Title

In Lesson 3, I spoke about Keywords and how important they are in bringing search engine traffic to your website. Keywords are the free marketing tools you can use EVERYWHERE in your blog post, and yet many people don't.

Titles are a great place for keywords because it's the first thing the Search Engine Spiders look through when they come to your site. However, people are a little bit different than spiders, so you have to be more creative when it comes to making titles for humans.

By E.T. Barton

Keywords are a good thing, but copy is important as well.

Here's what you need to keep in mind when creating titles. The articles that get clicked on most often are "How-To" articles and "List" articles. People like step-by-step instructions, and they like lists. By choosing a title like "How to Make Money with Your Writer's Blog", someone surfing the internet who comes across that title is going to get a good idea of what they're about to find when they click on that heading. In the same way, a post like "Seven Ways to Get and Keep Your Readers' Attention" lets the reader know what they're about to find and that it's going to be "skimmable." Both concepts will make people click on the article if for no other reason than to see if they're about to learn anything new.

You can play up to that.

Another thing you need to keep in mind when creating a title is that free tweeting tools (which we will get into during the Twitter lesson) will take the title of your blog and use that as a post on Twitter. If that title is boring, people won't click on it. If that title offers an

By E.T. Barton

intriguing concept or piece of information, then you can get thousands of hits instantly. With Twitter, the title is basically your only marketing tool...so make it a good one.

(At the end of the assignment, there is a fantastic article that I copied from www.CopyBlogger.com about creating eye-catching titles. Make sure you read it.)

Again - a FANTASTIC Title Tool Plug-In: If you really want to make titling your blogs easy AND you want to drive traffic to your site, I recommend the ***Keyword Winner Plug-In*** again. It does suck that it costs $47 for one website and $97 for unlimited websites BUT, it can save you tons of research time.

2. *The First Paragraph*

Once you've created your title, the second most important item in your blog is your first paragraph. Not only should your first paragraph be loaded with keywords for the Search Engine spiders, but it should also be attention grabbing for the humans coming to your site. You want your first sentence to be something that reflects what the article is about, while also reflecting a bit of who you are. It can be funny, or pose a question – it can be challenging, or just downright obnoxious. But either way, a drab first sentence is going to make a reader bounce. So have fun with your first paragraph, and get funky.

3. Pictures

I'm always amazed when I come to a blog and there are NO pictures. When all I see is a huge body of text, I bounce – and so will your readers. I mean seriously...looking at a white screen and seeing nothing but words often makes my eyes cross, and I have to force myself to focus on what I'm reading. If I have to focus, then I'm bored

and I'm gone. Think about it...think about what attracts you to your favorite sites. Remember, reading on the internet is NOT like reading a book in your hand. People need visual breaks to keep going.

Therefore, once you've written something and posted it, take an extra minute or two and find some type of picture that is relevant to your blog post's concept. The funnier it is, or the more attractive, the more intrigued people will be about what your blog post is about and the longer they'll stay. The longer they stay, the more they'll read. Once they've read a certain amount of your blog and decided they like that article, they'll click on other articles you have to see if what they're reading is consistent on your blog, or just a one-time fluke. So add some pizzazz – a bit of visual color – with EVERY blog post you create.

- To get free pictures you can use, check out sxc.hu and flickr.com. Most of the pictures on these sites are "Royalty Free" (which means you can use them in newsletters and on blogs – but NOT in anything you get paid for...like eBooks or regular books) – and in many cases, all you have to do is let the photographer know you used their picture and where, and give them credit, and you're good to go. On SXC, however, anywhere it says "Standard Restrictions Apply" simply means you don't have to contact anyone or give anyone credit, but you can still use the picture for free. That is why I use SXC the most.

- A Fantastic and FREE Plug-In you can use that also helps with this is Photo Dropper. You simply type in a keyword phrase of a picture you would like to have, and it instantly searches Flickr for you. When it finds something and you insert it, it automatically posts credit to the corresponding photographer. It's free for the pictures and free for the Plug-in, so what's not to love about that?

- For cheap photos you pay for, check out iStockPhoto.com. The photos often cost as little as $1 to buy and use, and there are some incredibly beautiful pictures you can use again and again.

By E.T. Barton

By E.T. Barton

4. *The Body of the Blog*

Remember earlier how I said a blog with all text needs pizzazz? (If you don't, then go back two paragraphs and read it again...*sheesh*!) Well, a blog with a solid mass is another way you lose potential blog subscribers.

Let me put this another way. You know the expression "White Space" in a novel? I learned this from Trish Albright at a speech she gave at LARA. She said that when you write a chapter with a lot of action, you see a lot of "white space" on the page. That's because the sentences are shorter, and there's often a lot of back-and-forth between the characters. In other words, the white space is where the action is.

Now think about the opposite of the white space... the areas with lots and lots of words in big chunky paragraphs. Those areas are usually the description of the setting, and they can really slow a reader down. In fact, every writer should have heard by now how too much description will result in... (dun dun dun)... your reader skimming your book. And what are

By E.T. Barton

they looking for? The White Space. Readers want to be where the action is.

So why write big chunky paragraphs that scream, "There's NO action here!"

Don't do it. Instead, use double spaces between your paragraphs to make it clear to your readers where your paragraphs are. The more short paragraphs there are, the more the reader will feel like "This is a quick read...I can read this fast and move on." And that's when they're hooked.

5. *Subheadings / Lists*

Obviously, if you've given your blog post a "List" title, then you're going to number (or bullet) your main points so that you're reader can see that you've lived up to your title. However, in OTHER blogs, you should also use "Subheadings." Subheadings are an easy way for you to introduce different ideas or points into your blog in a clean, *Skimmable* fashion.

Look at this Lesson for example. You can very easily see all of my numbered subheadings, and you get a very good idea of what the information is in each little subsection. As a result, when you come back to this Lesson later to read it again, you can skim down to the sections that are relevant to your needs. In fact, you may have noticed that I've used subheadings in every lesson, and the only reason I've numbered these subheadings is to go with the title of the lesson. So by creating subheadings, or using numbers / bullets, you make your blogs more skimmable and allow readers to go directly to the points or ideas they find most relevant.

6. Blog Length

Another problem a lot of bloggers have is creating blogs that are too long. A blog that looks "too long" translates into "too boring" to an internet reader. If you want readers to read your full blog, try to keep your blog length to between 400 and 1,000 words. That's it. Any more than that, and your blogger won't finish that article. Anything shorter than that, you're not passing on relevant information.

I know what you're thinking. "But I often write more than 1,000 words. I NEED more than 1,000 words to make my point." Guess what... that's awesome for you because you get to create a...(dun dun dun)... SERIES POST!!! (Not Serious... *Series*.) If you find your blog is 1,500 words or so, why not cut it in half, make one half of your point on one day, and the other point the next day? You now have two blogs in one week for the price of one. Just end your blog with the words, "Come back tomorrow to find out why...(insert point here)". By doing so, you will have readers returning the next day to find out what the rest of your point is, or at least they'll return later in the week when they see your article in their RSS feed. (A second visit gets recorded as extra traffic to the Search Engines...get it?)

7. *Keywords, Keywords, Keywords*

Okay, I'll admit, keywords won't make readers return to your blogs or your blogs more interesting, BUT, since you're in your blog post already – setting up what I'm sure is a brilliant blog – you should be thinking about keywords (also known as "tags" or "meta tags") which you should see when posting your blog. There is NO limit to the number of keywords you can use for your blog, so "Fill 'er Up!" Copy any relevant keywords you downloaded from Wordtracker, Wordze, Google Adwords or the Keyword Winner and paste them into your Keyword / Tag / Meta Tag section. Because remember – this too is where the spiders will go to find out what your article is about, AND affiliates like Google *Adsense* (not Adwords) will use your meta tags to figure out what ads to put on your site, thus helping increase your income. Therefore, before you hit publish, make sure you have at least 15 to 20 keywords in your Tag section...period.

There you have it... Seven Ways to Make Readers Stay on Your Blog. If you have any further suggestions, please feel free to email me at Erica@ETBarton.net.

YOUR ASSIGNMENT (should you wish to accept it):

1. **Go back to any blog posts you've created that are missing any of the valid seven elements, and add those elements to your blog posts.**

2. **Go to Digg and look at the most popular blogs.** Check out the titles and see which ones grab your interest.

3. **Go to Twitter and skim through the tweets.** Make note of any tweet titles or topics that catch your attention. Most likely, if they catch your attention, they will catch someone else's as well.

4. **Finally, Read the Article below about Titles that I copied from www.CopyBlogger.com.** Then, if you get the chance, check out Copyblogger and see the mind-blowingly simple

information the guy has to offer. (You may want to print the list below for future reference.)

---

10 Sure-Fire Headline Formulas That Work

By Brian Clark

1. Who Else Wants [blank]?

2. The Secret of [blank]

3. Here is a Method That is Helping [blank] to [blank]

4. Little Known Ways to [blank]

5. Get Rid of [problem] Once and For All

6. Here's a Quick Way to [solve a problem]

7. Now You Can [something desirable] and [great benefit]

8. [Do something/Be] like [world-class example]

9. Have a / Build a [blank] You Can Be Proud Of

10. What Everybody Ought to Know About [blank]

**LESSON # 6: What Should You Blog About?
Finding a Niche.**

Now for anyone who knows me, they probably know that my day job used to be a Research Associate who specialized in Market and Financial Feasibility Studies. (I know... YAWN!!!... my eyes cross just saying it.) I bring this up because having been a "Professional Research Associate" gives me a big advantage when it comes to analyzing any market... including a writer's market. And would you like to know what I realized when analyzing the writers in

RWA? Writers are making HUGE marketing mistakes. Let me explain.

Think about this: Have you ever gone to an RWA Conference and swung by "The Goody Room?" Or...have you ever gone to a Writer's Workshop and received a bag full of "Free Crap?" (I know, I know... "totally harsh," but give me a minute.) If you have, then you've seen the hundreds of bookmarks and postcards writers hand out with every book they sign. On top of that, they leave that marketing material lying around wherever they think their customers are. I bring up the conference because – be honest – when you go to the Goody Room, you do NOT pick up every bookmark you see. Heck, you probably walk right by them in search of the Penis-Shaped Candy Tarts, and the little mini Sewing Kits. You could care less whose name is on the packaging...you just want it cause it might come in handy later (or it's fun) and then the name or the book title tends to stick with you. (Like the woman who writes the "Naked" series...I LOVE seeing her "Naked Reader" buttons at conference...very smart marketing.)

That's what I mean when I say writer's make HUGE marketing mistakes. They're all offering the same free stuff to writers who are being bombarded by other writers. The smart writers bring something different to the table(s), and people rush to see what that something different is.

In the same way, a lot of writers are writing blogs targeted to writers. And the problem is...everyone is doing it. It's as if those 10,000 writers are standing along a river, fishing for the same 50 fish. If they just went upriver a bit, they could fish in the ocean, and there would be a lot less competition.

Consider these statistics (direct from RWA's website in 2010):

- There are 10,000+ romance writing members in RWA.
- There were 74.8 million people who read at least one romance novel in 2008 (13.5% of all book sales).
- 29 million of those readers were "regular" readers.

- The average "regular" romance reader is a 44-year old woman involved in a romantic relationship.

When you take all of the above into consideration...why are all the writers focusing their marketing campaigns on selling to the same 10,000 romance writers? Why do they spend hundreds on putting ads in the RWR, which only romance writers see, instead of focusing on other areas. And again...*why* are they all giving out the same marketing materials – meaning postcards and bookmarks?

I'll tell you why... "Because everyone's doing it, and this is the way it's always been done. It's *easy*."

Now I'm not trying to offend any writers who use bookmarks or postcards. But I am a trying to make a point. My point is, *if you're planning on blogging about "How to Write a Novel"... you should go back to the drawing board.* There are already hundreds and thousands of blogs doing that, and the target audience is much smaller than most people realize. This topic is going to severely limit how much money you can make with your blog. It will also severely limit how much traffic you convert to email list subscribers. "How-to-Write" is a niche that is fully covered.

How I Made a Snooze-Fest Topic Like Bookkeeping Popular

I write a blog about Bookkeeping. As far as I'm concerned, bookkeeping is one of the MOST BORING topics imaginable. In fact, when I checked out my writing competition, I found a LOT of technical writing that literally made my eyes cross.

I decided to write about bookkeeping on a whim. I had seen a lot of businesses get ripped off, and teaching business owners how NOT to get ripped off was a fairly important concept for me. So I began blogging about bookkeeping because I felt someone should be talking in "Non-Bookkeeping" terms.

The first month, I got 1,800 hits. The second month, I got 3,600. The third came in around 8,000. A year later, I am averaging over 50,000 hits per month, depending on how often I blog (which lately has been once a week). It was actually around the third month that I realized I had something pretty good going on. People were subscribing to my newsletter left and right, and I was having other bookkeepers volunteer to write for me. My blog went from 3 million+ on the Alexa Ranking list to around 800,000 in just a couple months. That's a pretty big jump.

And yet...I still find bookkeeping boring.

To spice up my blog a bit, I created a fictional character: Betty the Embezzling Bookkeeper. (Isn't she cute?) To quote a reader, "She's evil, but fun." People LOVE Betty because I give her feelings and a  twisted sense of humor. I use my romance writing lessons to add a bit of life to a very boring topic. THAT is what is making my blog so successful that people email me and ask me for advice, and constantly remind me to "keep doing the Betty stories."

By E.T. Barton

How Will a Bookkeeping Blog Help My Romance Writing?

This is where Research comes in handy again. As a researcher, I know one of the most important things you can do in any industry is to "Define Your Demographic." We've already identified that romance writers are trying to sell to other romance writers. But the Supply and Demand in that pool is ridiculously skewed because everyone is fishing for the same 10,000 readers.

So let's define a new demographic. Who are the OTHER romance readers – the NON-writers?

- To start with, you know your reader is probably female, because let's face it, most romance readers are women. (More than 90% according to RWA.)
- We also know they enjoy reading – so they're smart.
- If you write YA, you know they're young.

By E.T. Barton

- If you write Steampunk, you know your readers like turn-of-the century stories with steamy gadgets.
- If you write Fairy Stories, you know your readers probably dress in Renaissance gear at Halloween and jab people with their "magic wands."
- And if you write futuristic, paranormal, Star-Trekkian stories, well I just can't help you there. (I'm a Star Wars Fan all the way. ☺ Except for the newest Chris Pine Star Trek, of course...what a babe! *Sigh*)

Okay, all joking aside. We do know that our readers are mostly female and of a certain age bracket depending on the story genre you write. We also know that they're probably trying to occasionally escape the drudgery of everyday life (because romance, after all, is an escapist form of art). We know they want to be entertained.

Heck...Let's forget trying to guess. Let's go find the numbers of who your demographic probably is.

By E.T. Barton

Want to know where to find it? RWA, of course. RWA posts all of the relevant Romance Writing information they can get their hands on right there on their website for both members and non-members. Check it out. Here is the site:

http://www.rwa.org/cs/readership_stats

When you're looking at it, consider your own readers and where they might be. How old are they? Why do they buy books like yours? Where do they read them? This is very important info any time you market to them – and what is a blog but a marketing platform?

My Demographic – the people who read the Bookkeeping blog – consists of bookkeepers, accountants and small business owners. Most bookkeepers are...*female.* And you want to talk drudgery? *"BOOKKEEPING!!! Hello!"* People definitely need to escape that. My blog gives them a chance to learn something new and have a laugh at the same time. And the best part is, I already have people asking me to tell them when my first romance is.

By E.T. Barton

They've also pre-ordered eBooks I've written before I was even done with them. How's that for helping my future book sales?

Your Turn

When you make a decision to start blogging, you need to think about who your readers are. What do they want to know? What are they trying to escape? What do they NEED more information about?   Because if "bookkeeping" can lead to romance novel sales, then whatever area of expertise you have to share is the one thing you should be blogging about. All you have to do is share it in a way that will get them to talk back to you. (That's the *real* way to know your blog is becoming a success... when people start talking back.)

What Are You Passionate About?

That is another thing you need to consider when blogging. If you're "half-assing" your blog (a truly technical term), your readers will know.   They don't want to read someone who is saying what everyone else is saying, and yet saying it with less pizzazz.   People want passion – and luckily, you're a romance writer.   Put your heart and soul into your blog.   Make it as fun and exciting as the book-of-your-heart so that your readers will be salivating to read each and every book you publish.

But most importantly, make sure you <u>blog in a Niche that answers a need.   The niche and the need are the keys to keeping your readers coming back.</u>   (Niche being a single topic, like bookkeeping, or Steampunk, or Women Over 40.)

"How Do I Know What to Write? And How Do I Know What My Readers NEED to Know?"

I'm so glad you asked.   It's easy.   Figure out what Niche you want to write in, and then start hanging out in the Forums.   Social Networking Sites like <u>LinkedIn</u> and <u>Facebook</u> make it really easy to see what your readers are talking about, and what confuses them or excites them. Searching for your niche on <u>Twitter</u> can show you hundreds of questions and comments posted in the last hour about your exact topic. And <u>Yahoo! Answers</u> – that's one of my favorites – is a fantastic way to find out what people are seeking answers for. (They organize it by subject.) Just search for your topic at any of those sites and you will soon find your mind snapping with new topics to write about.

Even better, any time you find yourself out of fresh ideas for writing on your blog, go back to those forums, read through some questions, and pick a question you can answer in a fun or interesting way...Boom...blog done.

YOUR ASSIGNMENT:

1. Sign up for your free accounts at <u>LinkedIn</u>, <u>Facebook</u>, and <u>Yahoo! Answers</u>, if you don't already have accounts. (If you have a Yahoo account already, then you already have access to

Yahoo Answers and don't need to do anything more.)

2. Once you're logged into those accounts, search for Groups that match your niche on LinkedIn. (LinkedIn is especially important...that site is gold.) Join the groups that strike your fancy. Try to stick to the groups with less than 1,000 people to begin with. Anything more than that can be overwhelming in the number of daily postings. Also, make sure you sign up for the "weekly digest" or you'll get 1,000 emails a day.

3. Look through Facebook and see if there are any groups in your desired niche. Join those groups as well. Read through and see if they're talking about anything interesting.

4. Do a Search on Yahoo Answers or Twitter and see what is being said about your niche.

And that's it...we're done with the Blog Setup Info. Lesson # 7 will be moving from Setup into attracting readers.

LESSON # 7: Step 1 in Building Your Subscriber List – The RSS Feed

If you want to start getting subscribers to your blog, then you need to set up your blog to start receiving them. One of the ways to do that is to use RSS. RSS is not really a new thing. In fact, you've probably seen an RSS Symbol on blogs you've visited before (picture at right). But a lot of bloggers don't know how to use it or what it even is.

By E.T. Barton

Basically, RSS stands for "Really Simple Syndication" and it's a "Feed" (like a New Feed) that someone can subscribe to. It sends the titles of a person's website to a reader's personal page so that they can see the last 5 to 10 articles a blogger has posted. On my personal Yahoo! Page, my RSS Feeds look something like this:

By E.T. Barton

As you can see, I follow several blogs, and I can see all of their latest posts on one page...it's very convenient.

However, there are now many other types of RSS that people never even think about. For example, Twitter and Facebook are two types of RSS. People post their latest thoughts, quotes and links to articles / blogs, and other people can easily follow them. That's the beauty of RSS... it makes following a writer easy for readers. The point of RSS on your blog is to make it easy for your readers to follow YOU. Let's go ahead and work out some of the various RSS feeds and goals to have with those feeds.

FeedBurner

While there are many types of feeds, one that a lot of bloggers recommend people use is Feedburner. Yes, there can be problems with Feedburner, and it is definitely NOT Google's best product, but it is owned by Google, which means you have the advantage of keeping

Google up to date on your blog at all times. Since Google accounts for a huge majority of internet searches these days, it is always a good idea to use the big guns whenever possible.

How to Set Up Feedburner on Your Blog

To set up Feedburner, you first need to have an account with Google. Go to Feedburner.com. When you're there, create an account. The best thing about a Google Feedburner account is that you can use the same account for Google Adwords (advertising), Google Adsense (making money), Google Reader (the personal page I discussed earlier) and Google Analytics (the stats on your blog). So while you're in Google, go ahead and sign up for the Adsense accounts as well, because you will use this to make money later on.

When you've set up your account, log in. You will immediately see a link to "Burn a Feed." The link should look like this:

Burn a feed right this instant. Type your blog or feed address here:

[   ] ☐ I am a podcaster **Next »**

Type in your blog address as www.YourBlog.com and click next. You will be then be prompted to name the Feed. You can leave it as is for the basic feed, or choose to get fancy. Here's that that will look like:

Give your feed its title and feedburner.com address:

Feed Title: | yourblog.com

Enter a title to help identify your new feed in your account.

http://feeds.feedburner.com/
Feed Address: | yourblogcom

The address above is where people can find your new feed.

Next »   Cancel and do not activate

You'll notice on the second feed address, there is no period between yourblog and com. That's important to remember later on when you're setting up the feed. Once you click next, the link is active...HOWEVER, YOU HAVE TO REMEMBER TO SET IT UP ON

YOUR BLOG. This has just created the feed, but the feed is not yet on your blog.

To put the feed on your blog, log into your blog account. Choose a Plug-In that helps people subscribe. (I like the "Find Me On" Plug-in. It's very easy to use and can  access tons of different RSS feeds. On Wordpress, to find a Plug-In, go to "Plug-Ins" – "Add New" and then do a search for RSS...the final effect looks like this:)

Once you've activated the Plug-In, go to the "Settings" Page, find the Plug-In you activated and click on it. (If you do not find the Plug-In under your Settings category, go straight to your "Widgets.")

Once it's open, type in http://feeds.feedburner.com/yourblogcom. Then go to your "Widgets" category, which will be under "Appearance" on Wordpress. It should look like the screen to the right:

After you've activated your Plug-In and gone to Widgets, you will find the Plug-In in your list and drag it to your "SideBar" (which is basically the one or two column you have on the blog style you chose).

When you're in the Widgets category and you've dragged the Plug-In to the Sidebar, you will then enter the RSS Feed (if you weren't able to do under the "Settings" category), or not. Either way, you will want to make sure to name the title of the Plug-In RSS as well, so that people will know what they are looking at when they come to your site. The screen should look like one of the following:

By E.T. Barton

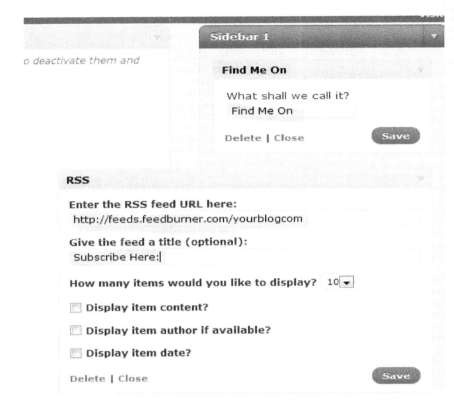

This top one shows what you can expect if you added your "feed" under the "Settings" category.

This bottom one shows what you need to add if you could not find your Plug-In under settings. Notice the website address in the top box... that is directly from Google.

By E.T. Barton

Once you've saved it, you should be able to go straight to your homepage and see the RSS right on your blog. If you don't see it, you probably forgot to save it, and you should go back and re-enter the information again. Also, don't forget... when it's up, click the RSS button and subscribe to your own blog if for no other reason than to make sure it works.

The Other RSS Feeds

As I stated earlier, Facebook and Twitter are also considered RSS Feeds, especially because people share their blog posts on those two sites. However, you can also add many of your social networking sites (like MySpace, Digg, Stumbleupon, Delicious, LinkedIn, etc.) to your RSS button, but again, that depends on the RSS Plug-In you choose. At this point, I will restate that "Find Me On" is one of my favorite plug-ins because you can literally add hundreds of sites, and many other RSS sites only allow you to add a few.

Either way you go – with "Find Me On" or without – make sure you only add the sites you are on the most. **DO NOT GO HOGWILD AND ADD 100 SITES!!!** For one thing, it will be too crowded on your blog. For another, do you really want to spend days and days updating all of those sites? Instead, just pick the RSS sites you use most often and enter in the web address to your Profile Page on that Site. <u>Definitely make sure to add Twitter, Facebook and LinkedIn,</u> because even if you aren't active on them now, you will be by the time I'm done with you. ☺

Quickie Links:

- www.Facebook.com/yourname (Sometimes, not all the time, you can put in your name after the slash on Facebook.com and be taken to your website. But it doesn't always work, so check the link first and make sure it's actually your site before you hit save. ALSO, if you have a Fan Page, use your fan page address in your RSS instead of your personal page...you can only have 5,000 personal friends, and an unlimited number of "Fans" on your Fan Page.)

- www.Twitter.com/yourID (Notice I say "Your ID" and not "Your Name". That's because Twitter only creates pages by ID names and not personal names.

YOUR ASSIGNMENT:

1. Go to Feedburner.com and sign up for their free Feed Account. Create an RSS feed for your blog, if you haven't already.

2. Choose an RSS Feed Plug-In for your Sidebar. Make sure you activate it and install it. Don't forget to enter the settings for ALL of the RSS Feeds you include.

3. Finally, test each and every one of the feeds. Click on them and definitely sign up for your own RSS feed on your Reader Page. (This will remind you how long it's been since the last time

you posted, and encourage you to get on a new site.)

4. Once you've done all this, you may want to make your "Reader" Page (or your personal page) your Home Page. That way, every time you log on, you can see your RSS feed, and the feeds of anyone else you are following. I recommend my.yahoo.com or iGoogle.com for reader pages, if you don't have one already.

LESSON # 8: Step 2 in Building Your Subscription List – The Email List

Everyone's been asking, "What about the Email List? How do I start one? How do I get subscribers?"

Before I get into subscribers, let's get our ducks in a row first. You need to set up an email list service for your blog, and then install it on your blog. While there are many, many companies you can go with to do this, there is only ONE that all of the biggest and best blogging gurus use and agree is the best. That ONE company is <u>Aweber.com</u>. (And after using Aweber myself, I have to agree...it's an excellent program.)

A writer on this loop recently stated that approximately 40% of her email subscribers actually opened the emails she sends. That's a fairly low percentage, and there are two reasons why she may be getting such a low number. They are:

1. The readers really aren't interested in her newsletters, which I personally do NOT believe to be the case. For one thing, if people sign up for a newsletter, they're genuinely interested in receiving it. For another, when readers lose interest in someone's newsletter, they don't ignore future newsletters...they unsubscribe. So if our co-writing conspirator has not lost her email subscribers, you can bet that her newsletter is probably not the problem.

2. So if this writer's newsletters aren't the problem, the other reason her percentage may be so low could be because of the mailing list company she's with. In fact, I recently heard online that a blogger who wasn't using Aweber had a similarly low percentage and couldn't figure out

what the problem was. Finally, they found out from another blogger that their email subscription company had originally sent out bloggers' newsletters as mass mailings (i.e. to more than 5 subscribers at once). When it was done too many times, the subscription company was labeled as a "Spammer" and blocked from many sites like Yahoo and Google. That meant that Yahoo and Google recognized the emails coming from the email subscription company, and automatically Spammed the emails, deleted them, or just blocked them altogether. (Now I don't recall which author said they had the percentage, or what company they said they were with, but I wouldn't be surprised if this was why her percentage wasn't closer to 100%.)

Aweber, on the other hand, has sent individual emails from Day 1, which makes them more successful at getting the emails delivered directly into Inboxes instead of Spam folders.

Now, I will admit, this lesson is going to sound straight-up like a sales pitch for Aweber. But I am about to tell you all of the things that Aweber can do for you as a blogger (and a writer) so that when and if you subscribe to an email list company, *you will know what features you need to look for.* Aweber is the only company that I know of that offers ALL of these services, and for the price that they ask. Everyone else is more expensive, or doesn't have the quality features.

"Please Confirm Your Subscription"

When I was at the RWA Conference, I popped into the Jayne Ann Krentz workshop entitled "Facebook, Twitter, and Blogging – Oh My". (Guess what it was about.) In the class, Jayne's Editor and PR person were with her, and they were talking all about how important it was to build an email subscription list.

"The email subscription list is GOLD," the PR person said. "And it will take you a long time to build your email list. But you can do things like have contests and give stuff away so that people will sign up for your email list."

Someone raised their hand. "But whenever I have a contest, I get the same people over and over who just want to win the contest. How do I know if the people are serious or if they just want to get something for free?"

I twitched in my seat, my mind racing a mile a minute.

"That will always happen, but just keep at it," the PR Lady said. "Your contests will draw new people over time. The biggest pain in the neck, though, is trying to get people to subscribe to your email list, making it clear that they are signing up for your list, and then getting them to confirm that they WANT to be on your list."

From the second row, I think I started rocking like a schizo. I wanted to yell, *"Are you kidding? It's not that hard. Don't you know about Aweber?"* But this was their class. It would have been rude to jump up and shout *"There's an easier way!!! And you don't have to spend money on contests!"* So I just took a deep breath, doodled in my notebook, and waited for them to get to something I didn't know.

You see, THAT'S the BIGGEST reason why Aweber rocks...they do all the hard work for you. You put an Aweber widget on your blog to get people to subscribe to your newsletter, and when people fill in the information, a little custom screen will pop up saying, *"Thanks...but you have one more step. You need to CONFIRM that you want to be on this newsletter. So please go check your email and confirm that you meant to sign up."* (Of course, it's not said in those exact words, but you get the picture...you can actually customize this message to say whatever you want it to say.) Then, the people go to their inbox, find an email from your website, and confirm that they want to be on your list. Once confirmed, you will get an email in YOUR inbox saying you have a new follower. All you have to do is create the message you want to go out (when you first set everything up), and then never think about it again unless you want to create a new message or a "Follow Up Message."

(And isn't that what we all really want? Someone else to do the work for us?)

Super-Easy Subscription-Widget Design

If you go with an account like <u>Aweber</u>, your widget is NOT going to be the same old boring email subscription box that comes with every blog. Instead, you can create a personalized fancy-shmancy widget with a picture of your book or niche that actually catches a visitor's eye when they come to your website. Since you want people to see they can subscribe, the fancier the widget, the better.

The best part is, if you don't have the "Computer Know-How" to create something with your book, you can pick from any of their super-easy standard widgets to design and create. You just follow the steps, type in the exact text you want, and then get the "HTML." (Remember me talking about that in an earlier lesson?) Once you have the HTML, you can go to your widgets screen and copy it into an HTML Plug-In, and bam, instant beautiful Blog Widget that makes people want to subscribe. (Look for the Plug-In entitled "Ads" or "Advertisement" for a very easy HTML Plug-In.)

Here are just a few of Aweber's beauties to inspire you:

By E.T. Barton

(Sorry they're fuzzy, but I figured you'd rather see a big fuzzy picture then a tiny clear icon.) So tell me, would any of *these* catch your eye when you're on a blog?

The "Don't Leave Me" Pop Up

Have you ever tried to leave a website and had a little Pop Up screen appear that said, "*Wait! Don't leave yet! Did you know about (fill in the blank)?*"

Don't you just *love* those?

Okay, maybe you hate them, but you shouldn't. What I've found recently is that a lot of those widgets will offer a big discount on a product that you wouldn't

By E.T. Barton

get otherwise. So make sure you read the fine print before you close it next time.

Anyway, the reason I bring this up is: <u>Those pop-ups will actually increase your subscribers by as much as 30%.</u> (The 30% is a quote I heard from another blogger...he said I'd get at least 30% more, and he was right. 33% of my subscribers consistently join through the Pop Up.) Imagine that. If you get 100 subscribers a month, then having one of those annoying little pop-ups can actually get you an extra 360 people a year (if not more). All you have to do is pick a widget (like the ones on the page above) and create a message that says, *"Wait...did you sign up for my free newsletter? I offer all the best advice on (blah blah blah) to my newsletter followers. Just click here and you can join now."* (Or something along those lines.) As annoying as you may think it is, I honestly find it works. In fact, before I put Pop Up on my home page, I was getting maybe 10 people a week. Now I get at least double that. So make sure your email subscription company offers the Pop Up feature, and then put it on your site.

(To do that, you create the widget, get the HTML, go to "Appearance" – "Editor" in Wordpress, and literally just paste the HTML anywhere in your blog's header or footer, like this:)

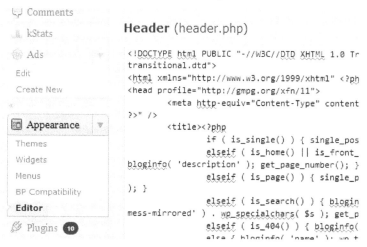

Broadcasts and Auto Responders

Obviously, one of the most important things with creating an email list is actually being able to create messages and newsletters for your readers without getting Spammed. As I stated earlier in this lesson, Aweber sends individual messages to each of your readers so that nothing ends up in a Spam folder. That

By E.T. Barton

means that all you have to do is create a message and hit "Send to All" and the message is "Broadcast" instantly. Just like that, it's sent out within whatever time period you state (meaning you can postdate when the messages go out). In fact, you can create "Follow Up Messages" two weeks later if you wanted a second chance at marketing your book without seeming pushy.

Here's an example. Let's say that you launch a new book. You could create three messages at once before the book comes out. The first could say, "My book is going to be on shelves on December 1^{st,} and I am so excited." Then on December 1st, "My book is now available for purchase. It's about...". Then two weeks later, "I just want to say Thank You to everyone who bought my book. The launch was so successful." You could even send a "Follow Up message" that says, "I see you bought my book. What did you think? Would you mind helping me out by giving me a quote I can use on my blog?" (People love to help people.) So whatever email subscription company you go with, you want to make sure it's easy to send your Broadcasts and Follow Up Messages.

Statistics

Finally, one of the most features to look for is statistics. You want a company that will tell you how many of your messages are being opened, and how many people are following the clicks. That's one of the best things that Aweber has to offer. In addition, if anyone marks your email as Spam, then it will show up in your statistics as well. (That's helpful since any message that receives a lot of SPAM hits will let you know in the future what kind of message to avoid...as well as what types of titles get your subscribers to open their messages.) Here's a glimpse of their statistics table: (Remember, this is early on in my blog.)

Broadcast Messages:

Send a regular email newsletter or other one time message to your list using broadcasts. Click "test" to send a sample newsletter to yourself prior to sending to your subscriber list. Once finalized, click "Queue Now" to have your message delivered on your specified send date. Split test broadcasts are available for lists with more than 100 active subscribers.

[+ Create Broadcast Message] or [Create|Split Test Broadcast]

Sent Broadcasts:

Results: 5

Sent Date	Subject	Segment	Type	Spam?	Sent	Bounces	Complaints	Opens	Clicks	Copy
08/25/10 06:42 AM	What's New at the One Hour Book	All Subscribers	HTML	1.7	259	2 (0.8%)	0.00 %	225 (86.9%)	61 (23.6%)	Copy
06/21/10 04:57 PM	Win Free Business Supplies for Tw	All Subscribers	HTML	1.7	201	1 (0.5%)	0.00 %	157 (78.1%)	27 (13.4%)	Copy
06/21/10 02:17 PM	Our First Contest to Celebrate the	All Subscribers	HTML	1.7	200	1 (0.5%)	0.50 %	256 (128.0%)	37 (18.5%)	Copy
03/11/10 04:05 AM	OneHourBookkeeper.com Newslett	All Subscribers	HTML	1.7	79	0	0.00 %	148 (187.3%)	116 (146.8%)	Copy
02/10/10 07:28 PM	How to Do A Year's Worth Of Book	All Subscribers	HTML	1.7	14	0	0.00 %	23 (164.3%)	19 (135.7%)	Copy

Results: 5

By E.T. Barton

Now that you have an idea of what to look for, make sure that your email subscription company has these features. By doing so, you will not have to work as hard as if you go with a company that doesn't have these features.

In the final week, I will go over exactly HOW to get people to subscribe to your list. This lesson is mainly just to get the setup correct.

YOUR ASSIGNMENT:

1. Check out Aweber.com (obviously). Their monthly price is only $20 a month, but you can get the free account that allows you to send 500 free messages a month (or 5 messages to 100 people, or 100 messages to 5 people...) AND REMEMBER – THAT $20 A MONTH ALLOWS YOU TO HOST AN UNLIMITED NUMBER OF WEBSITES. It is not one website of $20 / month.

By E.T. Barton

2. If you're already with an email subscription list, then check to see if they have the features listed here.

3. Whether you go with Aweber or another company, set up a Pop Up by pasting the HTML into the header or footer of your front page. (You do that on Wordpress by going to Appearance – Editor – Header.)

LESSON # 9: How to Get 1,000 Twitter Followers in a Week

As I stated earlier, Twitter is one of the most powerful tools a blogger has in his arsenal. Why? Because it's an RSS feed that many, many people are addicted too. As such, it can drive hundreds and even thousands of traffic to your blog every week. That is why I am doing a single lesson on Twitter – but it's going to be a detailed lesson, so get ready for it.

Let's Get It Started in Here!

First, start by signing up for a new FREE email account. I know, this is a pain, but within the next week, you are going to get 1,000 new subscribers on Twitter. When you get those subscribers, you are going to get emailed a lot by Twitter, each and every time someone follows you in fact. Then, many of your new followers will suddenly send you a "Direct Message" on Twitter, and Twitter will let you know by emailing you again. (Yay! So much fun... ☹) That's why, to keep from tearing your hair out, you're going to want to go ahead and start a brand new email just for your Twitter account. Of course, you can use it for your other social networking sites too, but I would definitely use it for Twitter.

Once you have it set up, you can forget all about it! Only send the companies that SPAM you to that email and ignore it. (I like Google or Yahoo for free email...you can access them from anywhere, and it doesn't matter if you suddenly stop paying for your internet account.)

How Twitter Works

Remember in Lesson 7 when I discussed the whole RSS feed...Well, basically, that's what Twitter is. It's one big giant RSS feed. In fact, it's an RSS Feast.

Here are a couple things to know about Twitter:

1. Adding Friends is super easy. In fact, adding friends on Twitter is easier than any other social networking site I've seen so far.
2. Twitter will show you how long it's been since someone's posted right down to the past 30 seconds. (I'm serious.)
3. There are three main lists in Twitter: the people

you are following, the people following you, and the lists that are following you. (See the lists in the blue square?)

By E.T. Barton

4. Twitter will only allow you to follow a maximum of 2,000 friends...at least until you have 2,000 people following you. It's their way of making sure you aren't just going to SPAM people.

5. Twitter was originally intended for teenagers, but it was actually business-minded people who found the biggest use for it. That means that most of your Twitter followers are probably going to be professional adults in your desired demographic age range. (Yay!)

6. People follow Twitter on their cell phones – that's how addicted to it they are.

7. With websites like TweetDeck, people can now see what all of their friends and business colleagues are doing right down to the minute they post it.

8. Twitter is fabulous if you have a question and need a fast answer. All you have to do is search for the problem you're having – or ask a question on your Twitter page – and people can get back to you instantly.

9. Finally, you CAN customize your Twitter settings to have a real picture of you, your book, your blog brand, whatever. Just go to Settings and click on the various icons there. You'll find "Settings" in the toolbar at the top of the page.

And that's it. That's all you really need to know.

Oh – except for one more thing. If you're using Twitter already to say stuff like, "I just shaved my legs," or "My hero is such a hotty"...stop. Editors and Agents can read things from your Twitter feed, and you're going to want to have professional stuff posted – not personal junk-tweets. (I'm just saying – it was another thing I heard people complaining about at conference.)

1,000 Twitter Followers by the End of the Week

Now for the juicy stuff... getting you 1,000 Twitter Followers by the end of this week. I know...that's a pretty big promise, right? (Especially since you're probably already on Twitter and maybe

By E.T. Barton

only have a couple hundred followers at most.) But it is possible.

Here's what you need to remember though. You only get 2,000 followers until you have 2,000 followers. That's it...that's all she wrote. So be stingy. Don't waste a "Follow" on someone who isn't coming back or hasn't been on in a while.

And you will only be allowed to follow 1,000 people a day until you max out at 2,000. So, you can 1,000 today, and 1,000 tomorrow.

Now, let's get to it (Be sure to read ALL of the instructions thoroughly before you go running over to Twitter):

1. If you don't have a Twitter account, get one. In fact, get two or three – one for your personal name, your pen name, and any branded name you want to use (including your blog name). Feel free to have fun with this. Since you're only allowed 2,000 followers (per Twitter account), the more followers you get on various accounts, the more people you will be able to drive to your

blog. Just remember, you have to have a different email account for every Twitter account, so make sure to setup any new account with new email accounts.

2. If you're already on Twitter, then you're going to

want to go in and clean out your "Following" List. "Click on "Following" and "Unfollow" anyone who hasn't posted in the last week. I know...it's harsh, but remember...you're only allowed 2,000 followers until you get 2,000 followers. That means, until you pass that 2K mark, you have to be stingy. (Besides, they're not on it anyway...they won't even notice.)

3. Next, you're going to "Find People." But not just any people...you're going to find the people who are looking for you and your blog. You will need to think of all the "Keywords" related to

By E.T. Barton

your niche. For example, when I searched for bookkeeping readers, I searched the term "Bookkeeping" first. Then, after I added everyone there, I searched the term "Bookkeeper", "Accountant", "Business", "Small Business", "Virtual Business"...you get the idea.

4. When the list of people in your niche is shown, go down the list and **add ONLY**...*wait for it*...**the people who have posted in the last 24 hours**. I'm deadly serious. You want 1,000 followers by the end of the week, right? That means, you want people who are addicted to Twitter... the ones who are on it all the time. To get them, you will have to be vigilant. Sure, you can add on people who posted a week ago, but they probably won't add you back until a month from now. The people who are on Twitter all the time are the ones who will follow you back right away. So go down the list and select everyone who has posted within the last 24 hours. Your screen should look something like this:

CGABookkeeping   ✓ Following
CGA Bookkeeping | Wakefield, UK
New businesses may be able to qualify for a reduction
of up to £5,000 of the employer NICs that would
normally be due http://bit.ly/dCnYAn about 1 hour ago

nalhbookkeeping   ✓ Following
NALH Bookkeeping | Burnaby, BC / Vancouver, BC
Mayor promoting Canadian green building techniques in
China: Vancouver mayor Gregor Robertson's green
business mis... http://bit.ly/92o9LI about 16 hours ago

BiroBookkeeping
Biro Bookkeeping | Temecula, Ca
biro 10:35 PM Oct 7th, 2009

JSMBookkeeping
JSM Bookkeeping, Inc | Miami, FL
A nice thunderstorm just passed over. I love
thunderstorms. Funny how little things can bring a
smile to my face. It doesn't take much. :-)
1:06 PM Jun 14th

a. WHO TO IGNORE: Be careful...sometimes when you're adding people, you may not notice that a year is added to the date. If a year is added, then that person is basically not coming back. I say that because sometimes you'll see today's date, but not realize it was for today LAST YEAR.

~ 127 ~

By E.T. Barton

b. Others to ignore include people who Tweet in different languages (you'll see them), people with NO date or time stamp whatsoever, and people who have locks next to their name. Don't even bother wasting your time with these people because again...your 2,000 followers are precious.

ibbkmgr
Bookkeeping Manager

5. Once you've maxed out on all the people you can find in your niche, search the niche again. Look for the person or company that you know is the "Head Honcho" in your field. When you find them, click on their picture to go to their profile page. Click on their "Followers" link. You are now going to see thousands of people you can add who are looking for your niche. Go down their list and "Follow" everyone based on the guidelines in Step 3.

a. For example, if I were to blog about blogging, Darren Rowse of ProBlogger is one of the biggest bloggers out there. I would go to *his* Twitter page and click on his followers. Then, I would go down the list and add everyone that has blogged in the last 24 hours.

6. When you hit 1,000 followers, Twitter will stop you for the day. That's okay. Just come back 24 hours later and continue on. In two days, you can add up to 2,000 people, and by the end of the week, you'll have about 1,000 followers. **You see, people on Twitter regularly follow the people that follow them.**

7. Then, in a month or two weeks from now, go back to your Twitter follower list and start taking people out. Take out anyone who hasn't posted in a while. Try to take out and add 500 people at a time. By doing so, you will have new waves of followers every now and then, and can hopefully pass the 2K mark within a month or two. Keep that as your goal... to pass the 2K mark.

8. Once you do pass the 2K mark, Twitter will only let you follow about 100 more people than those who are following you. That's it. Just keep at it, and over time, you're list will grow faster and faster.

How to Tweet Without Wasting Your Time

Okay, so you have 1,000 followers, but Twitter really doesn't interest you. I don't blame you...it doesn't interest me either. In fact, I think most of the stuff that's on there is crap. But like I said before, it DOES work in driving traffic to your site.

However, I also know it can be a huge time-suck, and I don't want that for anyone who tends to get sucked in by social media sites. So, right now, we're going to go back to your blog and setup some plug-ins to do the work for you.

Quick Note: *MOST OF THESE TWEETS ARE NOT AVAILABLE FOR FREE BLOGS. I wish they*

were, but all the developers are working over at the paid
sites instead of the free sites. So, if you do find a Plug-In
that works for your free sit to do what we are about to
do, please announce it on the loop.

Once you're signed into your blog, go ahead and go to the Plug-Ins page. You're going to search for any plug-ins that will automatically post from your site to Twitter, install them, and then activate them. Once they are activated, you are going to go to your Settings and enter your Twitter name and password. You are also going to make sure that the Auto Tweet feature is checked (if there is one). Now pick ONE Tweet Plug-In for EACH Twitter account you have. Anything more than this, and you are wasting your time.

That's it. Now, every "time you post a blog, your Tweet Plug-In will post a link to Twitter for you. Within hours, you should have at least 100 people popping by checking out your blog.

Some Wordpress Plug-Ins I like for this job include:

- AutoTweet

- Tweetly Updater
- WP to Twitter (although there have been some problems with it lately)
- **Tweet Old Post (This One is GOLD!!! It will tweet all your old posts, keeping your old posts fresh in people's minds.)**

To Get People to Follow You on Twitter from Your Blog:

- Be sure to go back to your settings and update your RSS feed (I recommend "Find Me On") with your new Twitter account ID... that way people can follow you from your site.
- Also, for a "Floating" Twitter *Follow Me* button, check out the "FollowMe" Plug-In. (Notice, there is NO space between the two words. That was done on purpose because there is another "Follow Me" Plug-In that isn't as good...so get the one without the space.)

Also, while you're at it, you may as well add some social networking buttons on your site as well so that people can quickly and easily share your post with other people. I like:

- "SexyBookmarks" (no space) for the bottom of my post. This one doesn't take up a lot of space, and has hundreds of SEO links.

- TweetMeme Retweet Button – if you want a count of your Twitter shares. (Note: this widget can be a bit depressing when no one shares it, but also exhilarating when people do.)

- 1-click Retweet/Share/Like – allows your readers to share your post on Facebook and Twitter very easily without being obtrusive.

One final way to Tweet without wasting your time – and to make people think you actually use Twitter so they'll keep following you – you need to tweet other people's stuff occasionally as well. This is VERY easy to do. 1) Whenever you read a blog you like and you see a "Tweet This" button, TWEET IT. (It helps that blogger.) 2) Go to your Twitter homepage occasionally and look down the list. Anything you find entertaining or amusing that you think your readers would like, "Retweet" that as well. (There's a tiny little Retweet button right in each Tweet's corner.) In 10 minutes, you can Retweet Tweets very easily. Plus, by Tweeting other people's blogs and comments, you help them out, which will make them want to help you out in the long run.

That's it. Follow this protocol and people will think you're a Tweeting Genius. On top of that, they'll follow your links to any other blogs you have as well, which could help drive traffic to any future book websites you create. It's a great little bonus.

YOUR ASSIGNMENT:

1. Create a new email and Twitter account if you haven't already.
2. Clean out your "Following" Box by removing anyone who hasn't posted in the last week.

By E.T. Barton

3. Add 1,000 people today who have posted within the last 24 hours.

4. Go back tomorrow and add another 1,000.

5. Install the Plug-Ins mentioned here. (There's no limit to how many Plug-Ins you can install, and every Plug-In can do something amazing for your site.)

By E.T. Barton

LESSON # 10: The 30 Tools Every Blogger Should Be Using

Okay, I know you're all anxious to start learning how to make money on your blog, but bear with me through one more lesson...the Widget Lesson. This lesson is all about getting the Plug-Ins and Widgets that are going to help you do more with your website without actually taking up any of more with your website without actually taking up any of YOUR valuable time. Some of these Plug-Ins and Widgets you may already be using (or I may have already mentioned), and others you may be looking for but just don't know it yet. Either way, print out this lesson and go Hog-Wild.

One thing to remember: Some of these might require you to change the "Settings"; some may require you to put Widgets in your sidebar; some may require nothing more than simple installation. Play around with them. Anything you don't like, delete.

Plug-Ins that Encourage Readers to Become "Regulars"

1. **What Would Seth Godin Do (WWSGD):** I love this Plug-In. It adds a cute little welcome message to the top of your blog when someone visits which encourages them to sign up for your newsletter. It even recognizes return visitors and allows you to customize your "Welcome Back" message.

2. **Subscribe to Comments:** Readers often leave comments but forget to check back for any replies. This Plug-In allows readers to subscribe

and sends them an email automatically when someone else replies to their question. This Plug-In will help you create Visitor Loyalty.

3. **Related Posts** (Helps Readers Find Your Other Related Articles): When a reader comes to the end of your post, they will probably want to read something else, but not know where to start. This Plug-In will suggest up to 10 of your articles that are similar based on keywords and meta tags. All you need to do is install it, and it will do the rest.

4. **WP Related Posts:** Sometimes if one Plug-In doesn't work, another one will. This one is a good one to replace Related Posts, in case you have any trouble.

5. **Find Me On** (I discussed this one in the Lesson about RSS): This is a great Plug-In for anyone who wants to make subscribing to your blog quick and easy. You can add tons of social networking sites so that people can follow you in their readers, on Facebook, Twitter, LinkedIn, Stumbleupon, etc.

6.   **FollowMe** (no space): Adds a "floating" Twitter Follow button to every page on your blog. It encourages people to follow you on Twitter.

Plug-Ins That Automatically Share Your Blog

1.   **AutoTweet** (Mentioned in the Twitter Lesson): Will automatically Tweet your Blog Post for you to whatever sites you want it to Tweet too.

2.   **Publish to Facebook:** Does the same thing as AutoTweet, but for Facebook.

3.   **Yahoo! News Feed:**   Submits your site to Yahoo! for you.

4.   **Search and Share - Text Selection:** If you're worried about people taking your hard earned articles and claiming them as their own, then you want this Plug-In. It makes sure that whenever someone uses your content, you get credit and a link for it. This way, you get free advertising,

By E.T. Barton

and an increase in traffic whenever someone quotes your blog.

5. **WP EzineArticles:** If you like the idea of getting your articles out there and having people publish them on your blog, then you will want an account with EZineArticles.com. This site allows people to reprint your articles (giving you proper credit of course), although you don't get paid for it. However, it is a great way to drive traffic to your site from other sites. And if you decide to write for them at all, you should get this Plug-In to allow you to quickly and easily post your articles to your account at their website.

6. **Tweet Old Post**: Posts old blogs to Twitter as often as every 4 hours. GOLD!!!

By E.T. Barton

Plug-Ins That Encourage Your Readers to Share

1. **Tweet Meme:** I mentioned this Plug-In before (in the Twitter Lesson). It shows Readers how many people who've Tweeted your articles, and offers a subtle reminder that they could Tweet your stuff too. Add this to the top of your blog.

2. **Sharecount for Facebook:** This one will give you a count on how many people have shared your Facebook page. I would put this one at the bottom however, since the next Plug-In looks best at the top.

3. **1-Click/Retweet/Share/Like:** Easy to share on Facebook and Twitter. It's also small and unobtrusive.

4. **SexyBookmarks** (no space): Put this link at the bottom of your posts so that when people are done, they are encouraged to share your blogs. This particular bookmarking program looks very neat and expands to show almost 100 different sharing sites.

By E.T. Barton

Plug-Ins to Make Blogging Easier

1. **<u>Keyword Winner</u>**: This will help you *as you post your blog* to choose keywords that will shoot your blog to the top of the Search Engines.

2. **Photo Dropper** (Adds Pictures): Remember how I said that you should add pictures to your blog? Well this Plug-In allows you to do it quickly and easily from Flickr. If you are writing a post about vampires just search "vampires" and click the one you like best. It's handy and saves a time uploading.

3. **Akismet** (Kills Spam): If you want to avoid Spam, you want this Plug-In. It's not perfect when it comes to monitoring Spam, but it does help by organizing them into an easy list, and deleting any that are a complete pain. Just remember – you need to get an API key to get this Plug-In to work. You will see the links when you go into your Akismet Settings.

By E.T. Barton

4. **WordPress Mobile Edition:** Everyone is reading on their mobiles these days – everyone. Make your blog easily accessible to iPhones and Blackberries by adding this easy Plug-In. It removes the clutter and shows your content in the best way possible.

5. **WPtouch iPhone Theme:** This Plug-In also converts your blog into an iPhone / iPod Touch / iPad readable version.

6. **KStats Reloaded:** A really good Plug-In for finding stats on visitors, spiders, page hits, and feeds.

7. **Clicky for Wordpress** (Already discussed this in a previous lesson)

8. **WP Super Cache:** This great Plug-In stores older versions of your blog to show to readers, which dramatically reduces the loading time.

Search Engine Optimization Plug-Ins (Your Free Marketing Plug-Ins)

1. **Headspace SEO:** This WordPress Plug-In is considered one of the best free SEO optimizers on the market. It's a good all-in-one resource for all your SEO optimizing needs – tags, analytics integration and of course fixing all your META information – in one panel.

2. **SEO Slugs:** Remove all the unwanted words like "and" and "a" from your permalinks so they are shorter and better optimized for SEO.

3. **Google Sitemaps:** Google Sitemaps will automatically generate a sitemap of your blog and its pages so that Google can quickly and easily index it (as can all the other Search Engine Spiders coming to your blog). This is essential for Good SEO (Search Engine Optimization) and this Plug-in makes it easy.

4. **Head Meta Desc:** I don't quite understand how this works, but it comes highly recommended. From my understanding, this Plug-In turns the first few lines of each blog post into different meta descriptions to also help Google index your site. It's said to be useful for turning your

excerpts on Google results into something catchier.

5. **Global Translator:** Translates your blog pages into other languages.

Last But Not Least – The Money-Making Plug-Ins

1. **Quick Adsense:** Install it for now – we'll go over it this week on how to use it.

2. **Advertising Manager:** This is ABSOLUTELY one of THE BEST Plug-Ins you can use for anything you want to do on your site. If you want to sell your books from Amazon, place ads, add Google Adsense, create a customized-RSS Box, etc...this one Plug-In does it all. All you have to do is "Create a New Ad" and then paste in any HTML. Once done, you can either put it in your sidebar or choose an ad from the drop down menu it gives you *inside your posts*, and VOILA!...instant perfect look for any HTML you

have to mess with. (I'll go into this more later...for now, install it.) Even better, whenever you want to change an ad on ALL pages that have that ad (for example, to put an ad for your newest book on every blog post), you would simply find that ad and then paste a new HTML in the space. Once saved, all of those ads are changed across your entire website. It's that easy.

3. **WP FrontPageBanner:** This Plug-In allows you to place any ad discreetly at the top of your home page. You can use it for Google Adsense, Affiliate links, or just to advertise your own books. It's a very, very simple HTML program to use, and thus worth having.

Believe it or not, you really only need three.

There are a whole lot more Plug-Ins you can use – after all, there's no "limit" to what you can and cannot do with a Paid Blog – so feel free to add many, many

Plug-Ins, even if they offer the same description. Often the difference is subtle, but can make a huge difference.

(By the way, if you Know of any Must-Have Widgets and Plug-Ins, please go ahead and tell us about them.)

YOUR ASSIGNMENT: *Install all of these and begin playing with them.*

LESSON # 11: Making Money Tip 1 – Google Adsense

Now I know some of you are going to say that you don't want to place ads on your blog because you don't want your blog to become obtrusive or too corporate. Maybe you think having ads will just annoy your readers. If you're thinking that, you may think that you don't want to do this lesson or the next week of lessons because you believe it won't apply to you.

Stop right there. You have to stop thinking that way.

First off, you're writing a <u>BLOG</u>. People know that means you are giving information away for free, and you will do whatever you can to make money in order to keep blogging. Your Blog Readers will automatically expect a certain amount of advertising, no matter what. In fact, if you polled them, you will find that your readers would rather you have ads on your blog so that you can keep giving them free information in lieu of not having ads and having to stop for your "real job."

Second, your readers are coming to you with a need for information. That information could be anything from "do police really call convicts 'perps'?" to "how would a woman in 1896 strap an airgun to her stocking?" They want to know what you know, *and then some*. **This is where ads come in handy – *both for you AND for them.***

On my various blogs, I have a few different types of Ads. On my bookkeeping blog, I put down all the best office supply coupons and bookkeeping software programs I can find. This saves my business readers a lot more money than they would find on their own. On my travel blogs, I put ads to the best travel discounts I can find. I also recommend websites that I know are good sites for information. ***In my readers' eyes, this makes me an expert in my field.***

And of course, it helps me earn a buck or two in the meantime.

So when you think "should I do ads or not", and "are they going to annoy my readers" ...just remember...this is another opportunity for you to prove you're an expert in your field, give your readers what they're really looking for, and make some money as well.

Why You Should Use Google Adsense

Google Adsense is the first way to make money when it comes to making money on your blog. Yet, a lot of people seem afraid of Google Adsense. They either think it's too complicated, or that everyone (absolutely everyone) is using it these days. The latter statement often leads people to ponder, "If everyone is using Google Adsense, wouldn't it be better for me to use something else?" The answer is...Google made over $19 BILLION in advertising revenue last year. Many, many bloggers got a fat chunk of that money. Why aren't YOU one of them? (If you're not, of course.)

Here are other reasons why you should use Google Adsense:

- Google Adsense is one of the only programs that will make you money without you having to do anything (other than place the ads). All you have to do is create a few ads, position them in a few discrete places, and you can start making a couple dollars every time you post a blog. While a couple dollars may not seem like a lot of money, it can easily become enough money every month to pay for something like...hmmm....*Aweber*.

- Google Adsense will TARGET your ads to your customers. They do this by searching for the keywords you put in your title, your tagline, your blog post, your categories, and in your Meta tags.

By doing this, it can suggest ads that compliment your information, thus *adding* to your blog instead of detracting.

- Every time someone just "clicks" on one of your Google Adsense ads (notice I say "clicks" and not "buys"), you make money. That is one of the best things about Google Adsense. Your readers don't have to buy anything. You get the money simply because having the ad on your site makes you a "lead" for Google. Then Google pays you for the potential income they could make from your readers versus the actual income they get make from your readers. Sure, it may only be a few cents per click, but that's still better than nothing. And the more readers you have that click on those ads, the more money you make.

- And again – relevant ads will allow you to help your readers, thus making your blog an expert site in their eyes. Why not get paid for being the expert you are (and for recommending relevant products)?

Before you can proceed, however, you must get a FREE Google Adsense account. To do that, simply go to www.Google.com/adsense. That's it. Simply sign up and link to any existing bank account for payment, or have them send a check to your home. *(Quick Note: You will have to pay a "Check Fee" if you choose to have the money sent to your home instead of paid to your bank account. It's $3, which isn't much. Also, Google will only send you a check monthly AND only when you've reached $100. If you're under $100, they carry the balance from month to month until you hit $100.)*

Blog Basics (I know..."More?"...*Insert Eye Roll Here*)

Okay, we've gone through a lot of Blog Basics in other lessons, but tonight, I'm going to talk about the Anatomy of a blog. The Anatomy is important because it can mean the difference between a blog that makes money and a blog that doesn't. So, real quick, here's your basic blog layout. (These pictures are straight from Google.)

By E.T. Barton

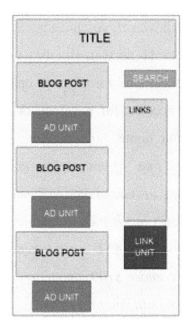

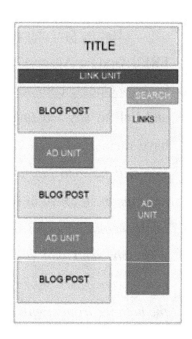

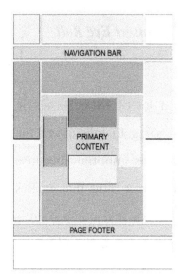

1. You have the Header (or Title) space at the top, where your Blog Title and Tagline go.

2. You have one main column for the blogs you're posting (whether left, right or center).

3. You have one to two

"Sidebar Columns" where you can put additional information (like related posts, categories, calendars, widgets, ads, etc.) Those sidebar columns may also have their own individual boxes, so technically, you could have more than two sidebars on your blog, all in a single column.

4. You have a Navigation Bar (or Link Unit) where your readers can link to other pages. (That navigation bar is either below your Header Box and above your Blog Post, or in your Sidebar.)

5. And finally, you have the Footer, where you can generally find information about the Blog Theme's Creator, Bookmarking Tools, Comments, etc.

All of these spaces should be working for you, whether making money or promoting your blog. And technically, any kind of ad can go in any of these locations.

By E.T. Barton

Creating Discrete Google Ads

The key to having Effective Google Ads that will make you money is actually to be "Discrete." In other words, you want your ads to "blend" into the article and your blog. The more your Google ads blend, the more your readers will think the information is part of your blog, and the more they'll be willing to click on any links. To make this happen, you need to:

1. Use "Adlinks" whenever possible.
2. Make any Google Adsense links in your blog match your "Other" links.
3. Place Your Google Adsense Adlinks in Discrete Locations.
4. Use Your Prime Real Estate for Banner Ads.
5. Utilize as many types of Google Adsense Ads as you can.

In today's lesson, we are going to discuss Steps 1 to 3. Tomorrow, I will go over Step 4 & 5.

1. Use Adlinks Whenever Possible

An Adlink is – quite simply – a "Text" ad. That means there are no pictures, no gif animation, and no video. It's just straight up text. The reason you want these "Adlinks" is because they are not annoying...they are very discrete. They look they belong on your blog, even though they have a little bar that says "Ads by Google."

There are two types of Adlink ads you want to consider. The first is a "Horizontal" Adlink that looks something like this:

Ads by Google   Ad Link Here   Ad Link Here   Ad Link Here

The second is a "Vertical" Adlink that looks like this:

Ads by Google
Bicycle parts
Bicycle training
Bicycle shops
Cycling news

You can use both on your site... however, I find that that Horizontal Adlinks work best for me.

By E.T. Barton

To Create an Adlinks Ad, you will:

2. **Log into your Google Adsense account.**

3. **Click on the "Adsense Setup" Tab, and then make sure you're in the "Get Ads" section** (see below).

4. **Click on "Adsense for Content"** (Looks like this):

Google AdSense

Reports	AdSense Setup	My Account	Resources

Get Ads | Manage Ads | Color Palettes | Channels | Competitive Ad Filter | Site Authenti

AdSense Setup

Choose the product you'd like to add to your site.

AdSense for Content
Display ads that are targeted to your site's content or audience.

AdSense for Search Improved!
Offer your users site search or web search while earning revenue from ads relevant to their search terms.

AdSense for Feeds
Place relevant ads in feeds Google manages for you.

By E.T. Barton

5. Then click on the "Link Unit" selection and "Continue" (See next page):

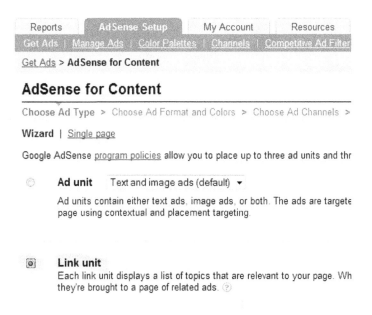

2. Make any Google Adsense links in your blog match your "Other" links.

By E.T. Barton

You should now be in the Google Adsense Wizard where you will choose the customized links for your blog.   Here, you have the options to choose the size, how many links you want in your ad, and the color backgrounds. (See the picture below.)

Wizard | Single page

You can customize your ads to fit in with your pages. Use the options below to specify ad size, style, and more.

Format

Link units come in a variety of sizes - view all the options on our Ad Formats page.

468 x 15 ▸

◉ 4 links per unit
○ 5 links per unit

Colors

Choose from one of our pre-designed color palettes, or create your own palette. Tips

* Some options apply to text ads only.

Sample
Ads by Google
Bicycle parts
Bicycle training
Bicycle shops
Cycling news

Preview this AdSense unit

Palettes   Bookkeeper
            Edit palettes

Border   # FFFFCC
Links   # CC0000
Background # FFFFCC

By E.T. Barton

The Key Things to remember are to **make the ads blend with your blog.**

That means:

- *NO BORDER. Make the border the same color as the background.*

- *MAKE YOUR LINKS THE SAME COLOR AS YOUR "OTHER" LINKS. By doing this, you make it easier to blend your ads right into your blog posts. (Believe me, this will mean the difference between pennies per post and dollars per post.)*

1. **On the next screen, create a "Channel" name to help you track the progress of your ads.**

By E.T. Barton

2. **Click "Submit and Get Code."**

3. **Once you have the code, log into your blog.**

4. **On Wordpress, if you've installed the Advertising Manager Plug-In, you should see a link that says "Ads." Click on it, and then click "Create New."**

5. (If you have something other than Wordpress, I wish I could help, but I'm not familiar with them. Try looking for any Plug-Ins that allows you to upload HTML codes.)

6. **Once you're in the Create New page, copy and paste your HTML from Google into the box, "Import" it, name your ad, and then make it go live.**

7. **Rinse and repeat.** (You really only need to make one of each type – vertical and horizontal. Then, every time you use them, Google will update the links with whatever the article is about.)

Once you've created an ad (or multiple ads), the next time you go to post a blog, you should see a Drop-

Down box under your HTML tag. Simply place your blinker where you want an ad, and select the ad you want from the Drop-Down box. It will put in an HTML tag like the one below:

Enter title here

Upload/Insert

Visual HTML

b i link b-quote del ins img ul ol li code more Ads1 Ads2 Ads3 Ads4 Ads5

Ads6 Ads7 Ads8 Ads9 Ads10 RndAds NoAds OffDef

Insert Ad... lookup close tags

[ad#Adlinks Small Business]

By E.T. Barton

And 3. Place Your Google Adsense Adlinks in Discrete Locations

The best place to put Adlinks ads are:

- **Immediately BEFORE your post.** That means, when you write your post, drop down the "Insert Ad" box from above, click your ad, and then start typing in your blog post. This will give the Adlinks ad a "Table of Contents" type of feel (or a Navigation Bar feel), and people are more likely to click on it.

- **Throughout your blog.** The nice thing about these types of horizontal Adlinks is that they make for nice dividers in your blog. They allow you to break up your points and ideas, and they blend in smoothly. The vertical Adlinks are like pictures, and if done right, your text can wrap around them. Your reader will keep reading and hardly ever notice them. (This also increases the odds that they will "accidentally" click on a link, which means you'll get paid for their Booboos.)

By E.T. Barton

- **At the End of your blog.** By placing an Adlink at the end of your blog, the reader sees that they can click on other links to find similar products or topics, and you get paid.   It's like a continuation of what you've just written about.

That's it today for Adsense Adlinks. Tomorrow, I will post the rest of the Google Adsense lesson, all about Leaderboards and Banner Ads.

YOUR ASSIGNMENT

1. Sign up for a Google Adsense account, if you don't already have one.
2. Start creating Adlinks and putting them into your blog. You really only need one Vertical Adlink, and one Horizontal...but feel free to make more if you want to see which one does best.

By E.T. Barton

LESSON # 12: Google Adsense Part 2 – Banners and Leaderboards

Yesterday, I spoke about the Adlinks portion of Google Adsense. As you can probably guess, it is a great way for you to place ads on your site "discretely" while also allowing your ads to be relevant to the nature of your articles and blog. It is a good way to target your ads to what your readers are searching for, without you having to do a whole lot of work.

As such, today I am going to continue the lesson with something called "Banners and Leaderboards," and then I'm going to get into the topic of "how to amp up your Google Adsense income." It's quick and hopefully easy. So here we go...

Banners and Leaderboards

You probably already know what banners are (the rectangular picture ads that so many sites have), but do you know what Leaderboards are? Leaderboards are as common as banners, but are mainly text with a brief ad description to tantalize people into clicking. Additionally, they are in a banner format, meaning they are rectangular in shape and often have multiple ads. Here are examples of both:

Banners

Leaderboards

Google calls these Text Ads and Link Ads. The only real difference is that banners are a different size than the Leaderboards. Leaderboards are generally longer. Just like with Adlinks, you can make your Leaderboards blend by hiding the borders and making the link colors the same color as your other links. Here's an example of what that might look like:

Ad Title
Ad text
www.ad-url.com

Ad Title
Ad text
www.ad-url.com

Ads by Google

The reason you should know about both is that these are a bit more eye-catching than Adlinks are, and therefore not nearly as sneaky. Their main purpose is to give the reader more information while making it clear that it's an ad. You may think you don't want to use these (if you are going the discrete route), but it never hurts to test them and see how they play out with your readers.

By E.T. Barton

Another thing to keep in mind with these, you can get them both horizontally and vertically, and you can create them in any size. Most bloggers suggest you skip the 468 x 60 size for the banners since everyone uses those as banners. They suggest you go for the longest size so that it looks like a navigation bar. For the Leaderboards, horizontal is also a good idea since it makes it easy to break up your blog-thoughts and stick these in between your points. The horizontal ones take a lot more "know-how" and "tom-foolery" to get them to look right.

Ideal Locations

When placing Banners and Leaderboards, there are usually two ideal locations to do it:

- For banners, you want to place them near the top and bottom of your blog. The FrontPage Plug-In I had you install earlier is perfect for this. It allows you to create banner ads (whether from

Google or anyone else) and all you have to do is copy the HTML and paste it into the boxes under settings. It's that simple, and the boxes will be filled on every page you go to.

- Leaderboards are good interspersed throughout your blog. You will want to use your "Advertising Manager" Plug-In for this and just drop it periodically wherever you have a break in thought or are changing the topic.

- The ideal number of Google Adsense ads is 1 Adlinks ad in the blog post (preferably under the title and before the body of the blog), three Leaderboards throughout the post, and the Banners at the top and bottom of each page.

- While you can use Google Adsense in your sidebar as well, I prefer to use Affiliate links there. You have a better chance of making more money with the prime locations taken by the people who pay to be there.

Amp'ingUp Your Google Adsense

Now that you have an idea of where to put your Google ads, let's talk about making MORE money with Google. These few little tricks can definitely increase your pay outs from pennies to dollars.

1. Blog More Often

In one of the earlier lessons, I suggested that you should blog a minimum of once a week, but you'll actually want to blog more often. The truth is, you will only begin to average about $1 to $2 per blog when your blog begins average 20,000 hits a month. That means, the more you blog, the more often you'll make money. With Plug-Ins like "Related Posts," your readers will begin popping over to other posts, which could make you even more money. You want to give your readers a reason to visit regularly, so consider adding a blog or two a week to make even more money (for a total of 2 to 3 blogs per week).

By E.T. Barton

And once more – if you are having problems writing articles to post on your blog, you can ask people to guest blog, find free blogs to post, or pay people to post regularly. Here are some sites to check out if you decide to go this route:

- Guest Bloggers
- LinkedIn (Leave messages in your Groups Chat Rooms.)
- Free Article Websites
    - www.ArticleCity.com
    - www.GoArticles.com
    - www.EzineArticles.com
- Outsourcing Articles:
    - www.RentACoder.com: Put an ad for 100 articles about "any particular Keyword" and people will send you quotes about unique articles in that topic.

By E.T. Barton

2. Use Effective Keywords

Remember how earlier we spoke about Keywords and how they can basically get you free advertising with the Search Engines? Well, in actuality, Keywords do MORE than just get you free advertising. The other thing they do is get you paid. You see, Google Adsense uses the keywords it finds on your blog to target ads to your site and thus your readers. Adsense pays a different amount of money for each type of keyword that it finds and uses, which could mean the difference between getting paid pennies and getting paid dollars. What they do is charge advertisers a set rate for keywords the advertisers choose, and then Google turns around and places their ads on blogs where the information is relevant to the ads. That means, if you should choose keywords that charge a higher rate to advertisers, and have little competition, you could make more money.

To do this, you will want to become familiar with Google AdWORDS (notice I say Adwords and NOT Adsense). Adwords is where the advertisers go. By using their Search Keyword Database and typing in your niche, you can see exactly what they see, and you can use that to your advantage.

To find and use this tool...

Google™ AdWords

| Home | Campaigns | Performance | Tools | Billing | My Acc |

Tools

Optimize Your Ads

• Campaign Optimizer
Looking for ways to boost the performance of your ads?
The Campaign Optimizer automatically creates a
customized proposal for your campaign.

• Keyword Tool
Build a master list of new keywords for your ad groups
and review detailed keyword performance statistics like
advertiser competition and search volume.

• Search-based Keyword Tool
Get new keyword ideas based on actual Google search
queries and matched to specific pages of your website.

• New Placement Tool (beta) New!
Try the new Placement Tool to find new placements.

• Edit Campaign Negative Keywords

- Go to www.Adwords.Google.com
- Click on "Tools" in their Navigation Toolbar.

By E.T. Barton

Keyword	Monthly searches ↓	Competition	Sugg. bid
bookkeeping	23,000		$4.28
bookkeeping services	4,400		$3.91
bookkeeping courses	3,500		$5.82
bookkeeping software	3,500		$5.38
bookkeeping jobs	2,300		$2.43
online bookkeeping	1,200		$4.63
small business bookkeeping	820		$5.41
bookkeeping business	820		$3.54
bookkeeping training	660		$5.33
accounting bookkeeping	660		$3.32
outsource bookkeeping	660		$6.36
learn bookkeeping	440		$4.12
bookkeeping for dummies	440		$2.85
bookkeeping from home	440		$2.83
bookkeeping programs	350		$5.97

Save to draft Export ▾

By E.T. Barton

- Click on "Search-Based Keyword Tool". This will take you to a new screen.
- When you scroll down on the new screen, you will see two options. One will ask you for your website's address, while the other will ask you for the keywords you are searching for. Pick a box to fill in, and then hit enter. By doing so, you will be shown the Advertiser's pricing list.
- As an example, I typed in "Bookkeeping" in the Keyword box and this is what was shown to me:

You can see from this chart that people search the expression "Bookkeeping" 23,000 times a MONTH. In the next column, you see a bar. That bar shows the advertiser's competition when it comes to placing an ad. There is a lot of competition, but not nearly as much as the expression "Bookkeeping Courses," which has fewer searches. That means that Google is going to charge advertisers MORE to advertise with the term "Bookkeeping Courses" then "Bookkeeping". Thus, if I use the Keywords "Bookkeeping Courses" in my title,

By E.T. Barton

meta tags, or the first paragraph of my blog, I increase the chance of having those ads used on my blog, and I increase the potential income I can make.

Keep in mind...that does NOT Google will pay me $5.82 if someone clicks on a "Bookkeeping Course" Google ad. In actuality, I would get $0.05 or $0.06 per click, maybe less. Google keeps a LOT of what they make. Still, $0.05 or $0.06 per click would be better than $0.04 per click I'd probably get with just "bookkeeping" alone.

Now, while this may seem like chump change, keep in mind, you will probably be getting 10-20,000 hits on your blog per month if you do everything right. That can easily add up to an extra $20 or more per month in no time – and the longer you do it, the more this will grow. Google Adsense has a snowball effect, where it starts off small, but continually grows.

Use Ads, Ads and More Ads

Google Adsense allows you to have a maximum of 10 Adsense ads on your blog. That means, should you happen to place more than 10 Adsense ads on any page of your blog (including those in the Sidebars, Headers and Footers), Google will simply make anything over 10 "disappear." In other words, they just won't show those ads. It won't be obvious that an ad belongs there, but it can change your margins a bit if you happen to go overboard. The ads they choose to leave behind...will usually be the ones closest to the top of the articles and pages.

The only place this really makes a difference is on your homepage. Say you have five Google Adsense ads per post IN your post and your homepage shows your five most recent posts. That's a total of 25 ads, but Google will only show 10 – which will probably be all of the ads in your first post, any ads in your header and sidebar, and then the remaining ads in the second post. However, when your readers click on your posts to go directly to that post, then they will see all five of the ads you originally place, plus whatever ads are in your header, footer and sidebars.

Having said that, it is never a bad idea to use your full quote of ads. (See my recommendations above.)

Warning about Google Adsense

Okay, now I'm going to give you a couple of warning about using Google Adsense. You see, Google has some rules of usage, and if they find you are breaking these rules, they WILL shut down your account. I have found from other bloggers that should this happen to you – that Google suddenly blocks your account – have no fear. You can try to resolve the issue with Google, or you can just create a whole new Google Adsense account with a whole new email (perhaps the email you set up for Twitter). If you do create a new account, you have to recreate your Google Adsense ads, but then all you need to do is go into your "Advertising Manager" account and edit your old ads. Paste your new code in place of the old code, and every single one of your blogs will be updated automatically. *(Great way to change any ads that aren't working for you, by the way.)*

Therefore, here's what NOT to do with Google Adsense ads:

1. Whatever you do, do NOT ask your readers to click on your Google Adsense ads. Google considers this a BIG no-no, and since they send out "Spiders" to search your site regularly, they will find out. Just put the ads on your site and leave them be.

2. Do NOT click on the ads yourself a bunch of times hoping to up your income. Again, Google monitors this kind of behavior and they will block you. Only click the ads if you're genuinely interested in learning more about what they're advertising.

That's it. From what I understand, everything else is fair game.

YOUR ASSIGNMENT

1. Go back to Google and start looking at the Leaderboard features. You want "Horizontal" ads for the body of your ad, and 90x90 for any sidebars.

2. Check out Google's Adwords for your niche and get an idea of what advertisers are paying. Remember to download those keywords and use them regularly in the titles, meta tags, and the first paragraphs of your blog posts.

By E.T. Barton

LESSON # 13: How Would You Like to Earn Your $20 Workshop Fee Back?

I bet that title caught your attention, didn't it?

Well guess what...I'm deadly serious.   How would you like to earn your $20 Workshop fee back? For anyone who paid $15 for the workshop, you stand to profit $5 for taking this workshop.

Are you intrigued?

All you have to do is click on the link in this lesson (see instructions below) to go to ODesk.com or Elance.com. Sign up for an account (it's free at ODesk and $10 at Elance – which they credit to your account), and then post a job that you would like to hire help for. <u>You do NOT actually have to hire anyone</u>, but it's a really good way to see how cheap you can get really quality help and work done through the internet – and to open your mind to what could be possible when you hire the right people. I believe it's important to at least be aware of your options, and you the best way for that to happen is to check the place out from inside. These places will find you assistants from anywhere in the world for as low as $3 an hour. (I'm serious.)

I have actually used <u>Elance.com</u> to get tons of graphic art that I now own the copyrights to for only $35 per picture. That's a fantastic deal for graphic art that I can now SELL on any of my websites, books, brochures, etc.

If you sign up for both, I will give you $40 back.

Some jobs you could advertise for include:

<u>By E.T. Barton</u>

- Graphic Designer (for a Logo, book cover or advertising materials)
- Website Designer (for a new look to your blog, in case you don't see one you like among the free ones)
- SEO Submission (to submit your sites to as many Search Engines as possible, thus helping your site with search engine traffic later on)
- Social Networking (maybe to help you "Follow" people on Twitter or get friends on both LinkedIn, Facebook or even MySpace)
- Ghost or Guest Blogging (hire someone to write a certain number of blog posts for you – claim them as your own or give credit where credit is due)
- Research (we all need that, whether for our blogs or our books)
- Editing and/or Proofreading (again – what writer doesn't need that)

Those are just some ideas to get you started.

The Instructions to Make Your $20 (or $40) Back

Okay, to do this right, so that you qualify to make your $20 (or $40) back, just do the following:

1. **Click Here to go to ODesk.com or Elance.com.** You have to click on this link in this PDF in order for it to work. If you go straight to the website, I won't get credited with "leading" you to their site.

   a. If you can't click on the link, then enter the following website code into your address bar:

      i. **ODesk.com: http://www.anrdoezrs.net/click-2775681-10715495**

      ii. **Elance: http://www.anrdoezrs.net/click-3990205-10777892**

2. **Sign up for a NEW Account and pay the $10 registration fee.** Again, it has to be a NEW account to get credit. If you already have an Elance account, just create a new account with a new email address and you will qualify for the $20.

3. **Post a new job.** The job can be absolutely anything you like. The point is to get quotes for something you might have tried doing all by your lonesome.

4. **Once the job has been posted, email me the link to the posting at <u>Erica@ETBarton.net</u>.** By this, all I mean is to open an email, copy and paste the "http://" address of the page your posting is on and send it to me.

5. **In the email you send me, be sure to include your PayPal email address so that I can pay you.** You have to have a Paypal account in order to qualify for this offer since that is the safest way for me to pay you (for both of us). So if you didn't have one, you should get one of those too. Paypal will

actually make earning money on your blog easier later on.

6. **That's it. Within 45 days, I will send the $20 (or $40) to your Paypal account.** You don't have to hire anyone, but I do encourage you to at least look at your offers in about a week or so.

The Extra Bonuses

- Just as an added bonus, should you post more than one job posting at Elance.com, **I will pay you an additional $1 for each job you post, but only up to 5 jobs and $5.** Just send me the links to those as well.

- **Also, if you do this by the last day of this workshop, I will give you another $5.** It will take me approximately 45 days to pay you because that is when Elance and ODesk will pay me. Affiliates usually pay "at the end of the following month."

- **In other words, Open your Elance account and post 5 jobs immediately and I will send you $10 extra to cover your registration fee.**
- **<u>That's a total of $50 you could make just for registering with ODesk.com and Elance.com.</u>**

Why Am I Doing This?

Two reasons, really.

One, I am using this as a lesson about Affiliate Income for you. I am suggesting to YOU a really great company that I truly believe in (and that I know can help you with ANY of your blogging and romance writing needs), and I am offering Elance.com a "lead" to someone who may or may not be interested in their services.

And Two, they will pay me for those leads, so I stand to make some money, and thus, they can be the ones that pay me for YOUR workshop. If they pay me for your workshop, I will pay YOU back. <u>The money does NOT come out of LARA's pocket, it comes out of</u>

<u>mine</u>. LARA has nothing to do with this transaction, it is simply between you and I.

Also, I'm doing it because I figured, "This is a workshop about making money. Why not give YOU an opportunity to actually make some money out of this workshop?"

Where is the Lesson in This?

The lesson I am trying to teach right now is all about "Affiliate Income." Affiliate Income is when a blog owner (like me) suggests a company/product they truly believe in (i.e. Elance) to their readers (you're reading my lesson right now). If the readers take action as a result of the blogger's suggestion, the company with the product will pay a "Commission" for the "Lead." This Commission is actually called "Affiliate Income" to the person who earns it, and the Company paying it writes the amount off as "Marketing Dollars".

Now I will admit up front – <u>NOT EVERY COMPANY PAYS SOLELY FOR LEADS</u>. Most companies want someone to BUY something before they will pay out a commission. But, Elance.com is a company I DO believe in and use often, and they are paying strictly for leads, not sales. They HOPE that YOU will actually buy something, and THEN they make a percentage of the sale. But mostly, they just want people to be aware of their site, and they will pay for those referrals.

Let me also point out, I am an affiliate to THOUSANDS of companies, but I am suggesting this one. I am suggesting it because again, I know what this website is capable of, and I truly believe they can help ANYONE, whether writer or otherwise.

Personally, I have used this company to find a Research Assistant in India who I've worked with for the last two years, a graphic artist who created my Avatar (at the right), an SEO Specialist who helped me get Twitter followers, a blogger to post information on my AirlinesThatFlyTo.com website, and an assistant in Australia who went Apartment

Hunting for me before I left for Sydney. Like I said, I BELIEVE in this company.

Picture by Rin Kuorhana

How Do YOU Become an Affiliate?

Okay, let's really get into the lesson now. You want this...you WANT to be an Affiliate. There is bigger money in being an Affiliate than in blogging alone. With Affiliate income, you can make anything from $1 a lead, to over $100 per sale. That's more than Google Adsense is going to pay you for a while.

So how do you become an affiliate? It's so simple, you'll think "There must be more to it than this..."

To become an affiliate, go to Commission Junction (www.CJ.com) and sign up for a Free account. (And by the way, I am NOT an affiliate of Commission Junction, but I have used their website for the last seven years, and I've made several hundred a year from them even BEFORE I became a blogger.) Once you've signed up, you simply begin browsing for companies or products you know that your readers are interested in. You "Ask" to join their Affiliate network. Many will automatically approve you, while others will take a week or so. Once you are approved, you can search through their banners, text links, and ads and find THE BEST deals and discounts on EVERYTHING.   (It totally rocks.) Remember how I mentioned in a previous lesson that you want to be "The Expert" on your niche when it comes to blogging?   Well, Affiliate Income is actually going to help you do this, and do it profitably.

Okay, I'm an Affiliate. Now What?

After you've signed up to become an affiliate, there are a few ways that you will want to go about making money as an affiliate.   Here they are, in no particular order, and here's how they can make you money:

- **Your Job:** This is an obvious way and may not be exactly what you're looking for, but it DOES work. The next time you're at work, keep your ears open. Anytime you hear someone say, "I'm looking for a deal on..." that's when you will speak up. You can say, "Hey, why don't you let me look into it. I have some sites I can check, and I could find you something pretty quick. Just give me an hour." Once they've agreed, all you have to do is go to <u>CJ.com</u> account and "Find Links" for whatever "Product" that person is looking for. You can then sort them by retail price or commission, get the HTML, follow your special website code to your affiliate's link, and then make the purchase (or send the link to your boss/co-worker). Just like that, you've made an extra cash bonus just for being alert and using your connections.

- **Your Blog's Home Page:** Once you've chosen a few affiliates you believe in, get the HTML and put it into your "Advertising Manager" Plug-In. Then, place the "Advertising Manager" Widgets into your sidebar, and possibly your FrontPage Plug-In (if you want it to be at the top or bottom of your site). Six in the Sidebar (all in a row for a cleaner look) and one at the top and bottom are usually a good number of Links to have without making your page look too cluttered.

- **Your Blog Posts:** When you write any kind of blog post that gives a "Glowing Review" to something, check and see if there are any affiliate links that match up with your topic. Pick random words throughout your blog post related to that topic, and then link it to your special affiliate code from Commission Junction. When someone clicks on that link, you could make a sale if you get paid for links, or a commission if a sale happens.

- **A Dedicated Blog Page:** It never hurts to create an individual page with coupons and links to some of your affiliates and their "Deals". By doing so, you make those products and companies easy to find later on, and you give your readers a place to go to find those deals as well. It's a win-win.

- **Your Newsletter:** This is one of the main reasons you want a email newsletter subscription list. If you have a newsletter with subscribers, you have people who WANT you to tell them what's going on with you and your site. You can put ads discretely throughout your newsletter, or you can be bold and encourage them to check out the latest affiliate deal for the month. Both ways will help you make money, and both ways can set you apart as an expert.

- **Yourself:** And let me just point out...you make a commission every time YOU buy from your own links. For example, take my trip around the world. I'm using my affiliate connections to find the best prices on hotels, cars, and flights. I find the advertised deals at my favorite sites every month, then place links on my blog so I can find them again later. Then, every time I need to book something, I go back to my blog, click on the link, and make $5 to $10 back for each

By E.T. Barton

booking. So far, I've made about $300 back just from travelling – money I would have thrown away if I weren't an affiliate.

Other Affiliate Companies / Products

While there are many other Affiliate companies out there, there is only one more that I've heard bloggers talking about. That one is ClickBank.com. (Again, I'm not an affiliate, but I do have an account there to access their products.) Clickbank is basically a company where you can go and get links to sell digital products you might believe in. There are eBooks and videos there, and the commission is up to 75% of any sales. You just browse their products, place a link or two as mentioned above, and then you can make anywhere from $5 to hundreds for the sale of one individual product. What's not to love about that?

By the way, this is an EXCELLENT place to advertise your own digital products, if and when the time comes. Why not have someone become YOUR affiliate as well?

I Don't Understand the HTML Codes on the Site

Here's a quick rundown on the HTML you will find at CJ.com. Once you've picked a product and clicked "Get HTML", you will be taken to a screen where your codes are generated.

The screen will look like this:

By E.T. Barton

Elance – A World of Talent Online Detail » Get Links : Text Link » Link Detail » **Get HTML**

Elance – A World of Talent Online: Text Link

Find a world of talent online at Elance Post your job today.

Link Type	Text Link
PID	3990205
AID	10777892
Web Site	Pro BizAssist ▸
Encrypt link?	☐ Yes
Set link to open a new browser window?	☐ Yes
Hide tracking code in link?	☐ Yes
SID	
Destination URL	http://www.elance com/employersignup
Update Link Code	
Code	`<a href="http://www.anrdoezrs.net/click-3990205-10777892" target="_top">Find a world of talent online at Elance </a> Post your job today. <img src="http://www.tqlkg com/image-3990205-10777892" width="1" height="1" border="0"/>`

Highlight Code   Close

By E.T. Barton

You would copy everything in the code box and paste it into your Advertising Manager in order to create the ad at the top (the line in blue). If you want only the website link and no blue text or additional comments, pictures, flashing gif, etc., you would copy and paste ONLY the http:// website code. You can "Insert" it as HTML if you're writing in Word, or you can "Link" it to a "New Window" if you're linking it to a word in your blog post. Copy and paste that code into your website when searching for yourself or your associates, and you will be taken straight to your commissioned website. It's that simple, and it can be very profitable.

YOUR ASSIGNMENT

1. Go to ODesk.com or Elance.com and make your $40 or $50 – but only if you want too. (Don't feel you have to because I'm greedy...do it because YOU'RE greedy. ☺ Just kidding.)
   a. Click on these links to get an account:

      i. **ODesk.com:**

        http://www.anrdoezrs.net/click-2775681-10715495

      ii. **Elance:**

        http://www.anrdoezrs.net/click-3990205-10777892

b. Post a job (or 5 on Elance to get your $10 bonus).

c. Forward your job link(s) to me at Erica@ETBarton.net. (Please forward them all in one email so that I can make one lump payment instead of individual payments.)

d. Be sure to include your Paypal address so I know where to pay you.

e. If you don't have your money by the end of the following month, email me again at Erica@ETBarton.net. I WILL pay you, and if you haven't gotten it, your email may have gone astray. (If you need to hunt me down, you can find me at OneHourBookkeeper.com any time. That

By E.T. Barton

is my main business blog. You can also contact me through my writer's website: EricaBarton.com.)

2. Go to CJ.com and sign up for a free account. Start looking for links associated to your blog niche.

3. Go to ClickBank.com and sign up for a free account. Start browsing through their products as well, just to see if they can do something for you or not.

LESSON # 14: Selling Your Own Products

So we've done some of the basics on making money with your blog – mainly Google Adsense, Clickbank, and Commission Junction (i.e. Affiliate Income). Today's lesson is going to be about another powerful money maker – selling your own products.

Believe it or not, most bloggers do not make money from blogging. Their blog is merely their platform to sell their true moneymakers – their products. Those products usually come in digital form (eBooks, videos, podcasts, PowerPoint presentations, and any combination thereof), but they also come in the form of

By E.T. Barton

services (membership forums, consulting services, classes/workshops, webinars, and speeches). You'll notice, most of these things can be done by your average romance writer. Bloggers set their blogs up to sell, and then use every opportunity to sell those products to their readers. And if they can do it, so can you.

Setting Up Your Blog to Sell Your Products

In a previous answer and question session, someone asked what a "Landing Page" was. A landing page is a very important concept because it is your sales page. It is a single page that shares information about a single product, thus encouraging people to focus on what you're selling. An "About" Page would be an example of a Landing Page since the only thing an About Page should discuss is what your blog is about, or who you are. A Blog Page should focus mainly on your blog.

As a writer, you should have an individual landing page for each and every book you write. On each landing page, you will want to display the following items (if you have them or want to show them...most of these items are "optional"):

- Your book cover
- An excerpt of your book or a "Blurb" about your book
- Your Table of Contents (mostly for digital products that teach something)
- Possibly a Mini-Intro to who your characters are
- Any reviews or testimonial quotes that people have made about your book.
- And finally, an option to Buy the book "right now".

Other things you should consider creating for your books (which can cost more money, but can also result in higher sales) are individual domain names and websites for each of your books. By creating individual domain names and then single landing pages, you have the opportunity to create a really spectacular display for each and every book you sell (instead of displaying them like afterthoughts on your writer's main site). Once you've created those individual landing pages (and really, you only need one page per book and not a huge website), you can link those landing pages to your writer's blog, thus increasing the number of cross links and raising your ranking in the Search Engines. It's a really great way to increase your site's popularity without spending a whole lot of money.

(By the way, if you're with a hosting site like JustHost.com, the site will let you park multiple domain names for free or buy them for $15, and will also allow you to create individual pages using their templates. It's easy to do and inexpensive, while also allowing you to quickly put up an attractive site for your books.)

Another reason to consider creating individual websites for each book – *and it's a very important reason* – is that you will want to market your book. It's easier to market your book on the internet if you have one page to send them too instead of a whole blog where they can get confused about their purpose for being there. By having a single website page for each book that has a minor link to your writer's blog, you can heavily promote that site, get people to subscribe or purchase your book, and then send them a "Thank You" email that encourages them to check out your blog as well.

In other words, having individual websites and landing pages for each of your book is a very powerful marketing tool that will allow you to promote both your books and your blog.

For Those Authors Who Aren't Published Yet (Or They're Books Aren't Out "Yet")

You may be thinking, "But I don't have a book to sell right now. How can I make money in the meantime?"

There are multiple ways to make money even if you don't have a "Printed Book" for sale. For one thing, you can create an eBook that teaches on the topic of your niche. As you begin blogging, you'll see that your readers will start to ask you the same questions over and over. Take that as a sign and create a 30 to 100-page eBook on the topic that keeps coming up. Or you can create a video, PowerPoint Slideshow, or Podcast that answers their questions. Once you have this item in hand, you have something to sell, and you can start making money.

Or, another thing you can do if you don't want to create a digital product of your own to sell, is to find someone else's product that you believe in, that helps your readers, and that you don't mind selling on your site. By doing so, you can often make as much as 75% of the sale, and still make money while you're waiting for your (next) book to come out. Just go to ClickBank.com and start browsing through their products. In no time at all, you could have quality products you're offering on your site, and you have something you can create a landing page for.

Selling Your Own Digital Products

Once you've chosen what products you want to sell, it's time to put it on your website. Create your landing page based on the criteria above (artwork, testimonials, quotes, excerpt, background information, table of contents, etc) and make everything look "Purty."

If you're selling your own product, the first thing you want to do is "Upload" your digital product into your "Media" section. In Wordpress, you simply go to "Media" and click "Add New." Then you "Upload" the product you want to sell.

After the product has been uploaded, you should be able to click on the product and find the "Website URL" for the media product. It won't be visible on your blog, but it will be saved on your blog's server. (Your hosting company maintains your blog's server for you, but you should be making periodic "backups" of that server by "Exporting" it to your hard drive periodically. Trust me, it comes in handy to have the backups in case something goes wrong with your site.)

When you have the website url for the digital product you've uploaded, and you've created a landing page, you are then going to pop over to your Paypal.com account and look for their "Merchant Services" link. *(If you don't have a Paypal account, get one...you'll want this for everything you do online! And before you say,*

By E.T. Barton

"But they charge a fee to get money" – it's a well known fact in the retail world that sellers will sell as much as 25% more if they can accept credit cards. If the 3% fee to accept credit cards will make you 25% more money, you SHOULD be using it...period.)

In Paypal, under Merchant Services, you can create a button to "Buy Now", "Add to Shopping Cart", "Make a Donation", etc. Simply choose the type of button you want to create, and fill in the entire form that Paypal provides (it's very simply and very basic). Paypal's form has three basic steps which are:

How to Make Money With Your Writers Blog 101: The Basics

PayPal

Log Out | Help | Security Center

Search

My Account | Send Money | Request Money | Merchant Services | Products & Services | Community

Overview   Add Funds   Withdraw   History   Resolution Center   Profile

Create PayPal payment button

PayPal payment buttons are an easy way to accept payments. Check the Website Payments Standard Overview for more information.

Use this page to customize your button and create the HTML you'll need to copy and paste into your website. Learn more.

Having trouble viewing this page?

▲ Step 1: Choose a button type and enter your payment details

▲ Step 2: Track inventory, profit & loss (optional)

▲ Step 3: Customize advanced features (optional)

Create Button

~ 212 ~

By E.T. Barton

1. Choosing Your Button
2. Tracking Your Inventory
3. And Customizing Your Advanced Features (see above)

- Under Step 1, you will name your button (by your book/product title) and create your price.

- Step 2 you don't need to worry about – you aren't keeping an inventory.

- Step 3 is the most important if you don't want to do a lot of work. Under Step 3, you will be able to send people to special landing pages for both purchases and cancellations. That is very important for those people that buy. Once they've accomplished their purchase, Paypal can send your readers to any "website url" that you specify. That "website url" can be the direct link to the Product you uploaded into your Media section. Just like that, they get the product, you get the money, and the only thing you've done is set it up correctly from the beginning. The page looks like this:

By E.T. Barton

☑ Take customers to this URL when they cancel their checkout

www.myblog.com/COMEBACK

Example: https://www.mystore.com/cancel

☑ Take customers to this URL when they finish checkout

www.myblog.com/MyDigitalProductMediaLink

Example: https://www.mystore.com/success

Advanced variables What's this?

Use a line break between each variable. The variables will appear in your button's HTM

☐ Add advanced variables

Example
address_overrid
notify_url=https:/
business_cs_er

Create Button

When you're done, click the "Create Button" button at the bottom. You will be given an "HTML" which you can copy directly into your blog and it will turn into the button you want. Just make sure that you are in the HTML window at your blog when you paste the HTML code so that the button will convert instead of remain in a text format. The screen at your blog should look something like this:

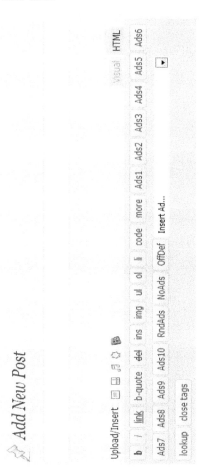

(See the highlighted portion?)

By E.T. Barton

To make sure the code worked, click over to the Visual Tab and search for your button. If it's there, you're halfway done.

Once you've got the button and the landing page set as you want it, go ahead and go live (i.e., "Publish" it). Just be sure to test the button before you tell your readers about the product. Test it, test it, and test it again. You won't be able to buy your product through your Paypal account because once you log on, Paypal will recognize that you already own the product and will thus stop you from buying it. So instead, ask a friend or family member to buy through the button. Create a new Paypal account just for testing and buy it with that account. If it doesn't work – which happens more often than not – go back to Paypal and create the button all over again. You may have to create the button a couple of times before Paypal makes it right, but it is so worth having on your site, that you should consider having to do it a few times as "standard operating procedure."

This is a really good way to sell PDF files, videos, PowerPoint presentations, podcasts, and "packages" where you create a combination of any of the above. For books that are published (and also come in eBook format, see the section below entitled "Selling Your Printed Products").

Selling Someone Else's Digital Products

If you're selling someone else's product, you create the landing page in a way that makes someone want to buy it, but include minimal information since the product's sale page is going to go into a whole lot more detail. "Link" the picture of the product to the code you receive from Clickbank (or the affiliate you're going to sell for) and make sure to set the link to "open in a new window" so that you're site also remains open on your reader's page making it easy for them to return.

Once that's done, periodically promote the page to your readers so that they remember you recommend that product. You can do that by blogging about the page, or putting a blurb in your newsletters. You can also actively promote the landing page online by paying for advertising (which you can do for all products and landing pages you create).

Selling Your Printed Products

Now we're going to get into something a bit trickier – selling your published books online. Someone recently commented to me, "I don't know if my publisher would want me to sell my own books...it might be a conflict of interest." I can honestly say in response to that – *your publishers DO want you to sell your own books*. In fact, at conference, that was all I heard the publishers say. Publishers were talking about how little money they can pay to promote authors, and that their marketing dollars are going to be thrown behind authors who deliver high sales. If you don't make your advance back, there is a good possibility that the publishing company will drop you. Therefore, publishers will actively encourage you to try and sell your books whenever possible (because they make money with every copy of your book that sells).

Here's something else to consider.

- The average commission on a printed book is 4-6%.
- The average commission on a published eBook is 6-10%.
- The average commission on a Self-Published eBook at Amazon is 50-70%.
- The average Affiliate commission paid to retailers (and blogs that promote Amazon's products) is 4-15%. (Currently, Amazon has been cutting off commissions to states that charge income tax on commissions. So, California residents are cut off from making commission with Amazon *for now*. Keep checking with them to see if and when they repeal that, or if the state repeals the tax.)
- And finally, I recently read a quote that Amazon sells approximately 90% of all eBooks at this point in time. Of course, Barnes and Noble is

By E.T. Barton

doing what they can to steal a chunk of that, as is iBooks (for the iPad).

Hopefully, you're getting ahead of me and can see exactly where I'm going with this. Just in case you're not, my point is – you should be an Amazon affiliate.

Being an Amazon affiliate has multiple benefits. For one thing, they can sell your books in both printed and eBook format. When you become an affiliate, you can create an "aStore" that you insert into your blog's Sidebar, or you can create a dedicated landing page for you aStore. In that store, you can add links to all of your books in all formats. You can also choose other products (whether books, videos, electronics, appliances, etc) that you can sell along with your books. By doing so, you get your normal book commission (as mentioned above) along with your Affiliate commission. That could instantly double the income you make on every book sold from your blog. What's not to love about that?

To become an affiliate, simply go to https://affiliate-program.amazon.com/ and sign up for a free account. Then follow the steps provided to create your aStore and pick your products. Once you've finished, copy the HTML from Amazon and paste it into your Advertising Manager Plug-In. Then drag the Advertising Manager Widget into your Sidebar and select the Amazon ad. The mini-store will show on your main page, and Amazon will rotate the ads for the products you picked for you.

Furthermore, you can create individual widgets for single individual products/books so that your products don't rotate. Once these widgets are up, people can buy from your site any time they visit. You can also put these ads on your dedicated landing page so that when people want to buy your books, they will be taken to Amazon where you get a commission on everything they buy during that visit. Hopefully, if your publisher has signed an eBook contract with you, your readers will be able to purchase the Kindle edition of your books and be able to read them instantly on their computers. If the books are only in print and not digital, they can have the books sent to their homes. It's a great way to sell your books without actually handling the money, and by recommending a company with a sterling reputation.

For anyone who's worried about "Best Seller Status" when a new book comes out, you can often get links to the page where Amazon will sell your book before the book comes out. Amazon will take pre-orders for you, and then ship the books so that they arrive on the release date. Not all publishing companies are willing to do this – and by getting the link and promoting it in your newsletter, you can have your fans buy during launch week, which is the crucial period for hitting the best seller list.

YOUR ASSIGNMENT

1. Get a Paypal account, if you don't already have one. Get a second one for testing your links when they go live, if you don't know anyone who is willing to purchase your digital products from you.

By E.T. Barton

2. Go to https://affiliate-program.amazon.com/ and sign up for your Amazon aStore. Then start looking through the site and picking products you like that complement your blog.

3. When you get a chance, create your aStore and put the links on your blog.

By E.T. Barton

LESSON # 15: Organic Traffic (i.e. Free Traffic)

Now let's get into the subject you all really want to know about: traffic. After all, traffic brings new readers; new readers become fans; those fans visit again and again; and you start making money every time they visit. To get into this subject, I'm first going to go over some of the Social Networking Sites that can help you get traffic. In the next lesson, I'm going to get into the ways that you can get traffic through paid marketing. (I know you may want to skip the next lesson, but its good information to have any time you want to market your new books and products.) Then in the last lesson, I will discuss the topics of comments and links. For now...social networking.

Sharing on Multiple Social Networking Sites Instantly

The biggest downside to "Sharing" any blog is that it can often take more time then you want to devote to sharing – whether your site or someone else's. (The other downside is that bloggers often don't make it *easy* to share because they don't put Bookmarking links on their website, should you wish to share their blog.) Thus, it can be a pain to try and share an article when a Bookmarking link is missing. But, it's easy to get around if you know how to do it. Here's how to do it fast:

1. **Start using Mozilla Firefox as your Browser.** Many people use Google Chrome or Internet Explorer whenever they surf the

By E.T. Barton

internet. But the truth is, these two browsers have more problems and create more problems then they're worth. Internet Explorer doesn't protect you very well from Cookies or Viruses, and Google Chrome eventually develops a problem with various blog sites over time. Mozilla Firefox, on the other hand, actually blocks a lot of viruses, cookies and spyware, is usually faster than Internet Explorer, and has awesome toolbars you can download to make searching the Internet even easier and faster. So, if you haven't downloaded the Mozilla Firefox Browser, do it today and start using it when you surf the internet. (It's free!)

2. **Get the Shareaholic Add-On for Mozilla Firefox.** One of the best SEO – Bookmarking buttons you can use is Shareaholic. When you download it, it places itself to the left of your address bar, and when you click on it, it allows you to share anything you find on the web at any of your

social networking sites. It's fast, easy and free – and it allows you to share even the most badly put-together websites on the internet. (You can download the link from: Addons.Mozilla.org/en-US/firefox/addon/5457/.) The link looks like the button to the left of the address bar – the green "eye."

3. **Once you've got Shareaholic uploaded, sign up for <u>www.Ping.fm</u>.** Ping.fm is a super-fast "Sharing" site that allows you to "Micro-blog" on ALL of your social bookmarking sites at once. It's free to use, and very secure. You simply type your logins and passwords for the various social bookmarking sites at Ping.fm, and then when you go to "Share" a site with your "Shareaholic Button," Ping is one of your choices and it will share the link to that

website page instantly. You're a member at 10 sites – that's 10 instant links to that website. Can you see how that can help an author very quickly with only a few seconds of your time?

4. **That's It.** Once you've pinged a blog article or site, you've helped yourself or whatever author's blog you're on! So add this toolbar button and start making it easy to share everyone's information – not just your own.

LinkedIn and Facebook

While it is easy to Ping all of your social networking sites with links to your blog, it is not the best way to share on LinkedIn and Facebook. The fact is, Pinging only adds a link from your blog to your Profile page at LinkedIn and Facebook. That means, after you Ping all of your sites, you're going to want to go in and personally share your posts on LinkedIn and Facebook. The reason for this is that LinkedIn and Facebook are fantastic ways to build relationships with your readers, and thus increase your traffic. Here's how to do that quickly and easily.

LinkedIn – The Money is in the Groupies

LinkedIn is a social networking site originally created for business people that wanted to network. One of the best things about LinkedIn is the fact that this social networking site has created groups where people can post news (i.e. blog posts), start discussions, ask questions, and even post jobs. A lot of other social networking sites do NOT allow this kind of blatant personal and professional promotion.

Yet as people became familiar with the social networking site, they began to branch out. Groups are easy to form, and with just the permission of a group administrator, anyone can join any group on LinkedIn. To top it off, LinkedIn will show you exactly how many people are in a group before you join. This is important because by simply joining one group, you can add 1,000 captive readers who will most likely pop over to your site regularly to see what you are doing. The more groups you add, the more people who you can reach.

On the down side, "Adding people to your network" is not nearly as easy as Twitter or Facebook. You have to answer a mini-survey on each person you add. But, if you join a few groups, you'll soon find that the followers will begin adding you – which can be a time-saver in the long run.

Some Rules for LinkedIn

Before you race over to LinkedIn and sign up for a bunch of groups, keep in mind...this is a social networking site that will email you regularly. When you join a group, you are subscribing to have all of the groups' comments, discussions and news emailed to you in a single email. If you subscribe for the daily email, you will get it daily. Multiply that by however many groups you're in, and you can see how this can quickly become overwhelming. In my opinion, it's better to join the weekly subscriber lists so that you can have a fast glance through all of the discussions are going on, and answer any questions that people may have for you or that you just want to answer. So stick to the groups that you really want to be part of, and don't be afraid to drop any groups after a while – especially if there are no discussions going on in that group's chat rooms.

Another thing to remember when joining LinkedIn groups is that size does NOT matter here. It will be tempting to join the groups with 10,000 or 100,000 people. In my opinion, it's just a waste of time. Yes, you will be reaching more people, but the facts are these: With 10-100,000 people in a group, there is a LOT of discussion going on. That means, it will be easy for your posts and discussions to get lost in the shuffle. You may find yourself posting and posting to the group, and yet no one ever comments on your discussions. That's because there's too much information in those groups, and the members will start to become overwhelmed and ignore the emails. Instead, consider joining the smaller groups (around 500 to 1,000). Those groups don't have nearly as many discussions going on, and this gives you a chance to set yourself apart as a big fish in a smaller pond. It will also help you build relationships with your readers, and the stronger the relationships, the more they will promote you and your site for you.

On the other hand, you don't want the group to be too small. Too small a group means you and the administrator may become the only ones leaving any kinds of comments and people may begin to think of you as "pushy." Stick the mid-sized groups where you can become just another active member.

Finally, a third thing to remember is that not all groups are built the same. Since each group is started by an individual, each group has a moderator that may or may not like you sharing so much. If they give you a hard time about sharing your blog posts, ask them what it is that bothers you. If they just don't want you to be so involved – bounce...hit the road...find another group. There are tons on LinkedIn, so there's no need for you to waste your time on a group where the members aren't allowed to share regularly whatever they want to share. Save your time and effort for the groups that are interactive.

Posting to LinkedIn

Thankfully, LinkedIn has recently made a delightful change in their "sharing with the group" process. If you downloaded the Sexy Bookmarks Plug-In, you already have the easy share button at the bottom of your blog. The blue tab with the word "In" on it is the LinkedIn tab. Whenever you want to share an article, just find the button at the bottom of your blog post and click that button. Once you do, you will be taken to a screen that allows you to share your blog quickly and easily with your profile, your groups, and your email list.

To share your posts quickly and easily (see below for picture):

- Begin by making sure the "Post to Updates" box is checked so that the link is added to your profile (for people that want to add you to their network to see).
- Next, check off the "Post to Groups" box.

By E.T. Barton

- In the category asking for the group name, add all of the groups that you want to share that particular article with. What I do here is click on the letter "A" first and see what groups pop up. I choose my groups and then go to "B" and then "C" and then so on until all of the groups are in. (It saves time in trying to remember all the groups I'm in.)

- In the next part, you will be asked to share a comment. If you share a comment in that box, then this Post will be shared in the Discussions section of the site. That means people will be more likely to read it and start a conversation. If you leave the space blank, it will go to the news section, and you have a lower chance of people sharing it or commenting, but it also pisses some administrators off less to think that you aren't just "Spamming" everyone. It's really up to you. If you think you can get a good discussion going, ask a question that's relevant to your topic. If not, then leave it blank and let it fill up the News section.

- Then Share it. That's all it takes. Five easy steps and hundreds and thousands of people will see your article in their email box within the next week (depending on which form of email they chose to receive).

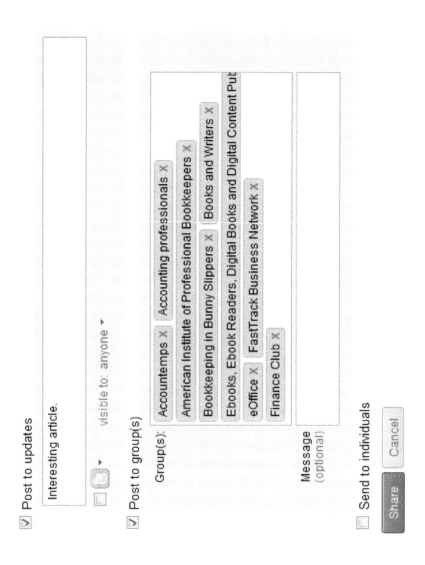

Facebook – Do you have a Fan Page?

Facebook has a limit of how many friends you can have. That limit is 5,000 people. Once you hit that, they cut you off. That can suck for readers that want to find you later. That is why you need a Fan Page, so that you can have an unlimited number of followers on Facebook.

Fan Pages are basically individual forums that allow you and your readers to chat with each other. You can share updates, and they can comment and ask you questions. A lot of bloggers love Fan Pages because it gives them an additional way to build a relationship with their readers besides just their blog, and it gives them a place to share ALL of the places they may blog at, which they wouldn't necessarily put on their regular blog. It will also help you build a mailing list so that you can email everyone at once (or so I've heard – if I'm wrong on that, please correct me). So if you don't have a Fan Page, go ahead and create one. Then visit it once a week to answer any questions and post your new blogs.

Tweeting

Do you have 1,000 Twitter Followers yet?

Whether or not you do, you don't want to become one of those self-promoting drones that only talk about themselves and doesn't help out other bloggers. While it may be tempting to do, people will soon notice your sharing patterns and they may drop you if you only promote yourself. Therefore, in order to make yourself stand out as someone who gives as well as they get, you will occasionally want to share other articles and blogs. The more you do, the more people will come to your site to see what you're up to. Further, by doing this, you can set yourself out as an expert on Twitter, and give yourself a bit of a reputation.

To do this without spending a lot of time on Twitter is a whole lot easier than you think. All you have to do is:

- Every time you read an article or blog you like, "Tweet it." Many bloggers put a Tweet button

By E.T. Barton

on their site that make this easy to do. If there's no Tweet Button on their site – because let's face it, a lot of bloggers *don't* make it easy to share their stuff – then go ahead and "Tweet It" or "Ping It" with your Shareaholic toolbar button (the green eye mentioned at the beginning of this lesson). Time Invested: 5 seconds per blog.

- Finally, once a week, spend five minutes on your "Home Page" at Twitter. From your home page, you can see all of the comments and share that other people are sharing. You can quickly and easily go down the list and click the "Retweet" button beneath any post and thus share their comments with your followers. It's a great way to show people that you're not just promoting yourself, and it only takes a minute to retweet several items.

Stumbling

I've mentioned Stumbleupon in the newsletter before, and this site is a GREAT site for getting visitors, although the visitors from Stumbleupon may not stay very long. People visiting from Stumbleupon are only doing so because they want to see something cool and are looking for as much interesting information as they can possibly get. Here's the basics:

- When you sign up for a free Stumbleupon account, you fill out a basic survey of what you like. This way, Stumbleupon will only recommend sites that are relevant to your interests.
- Next, they have you download a Stumbleupon toolbar.

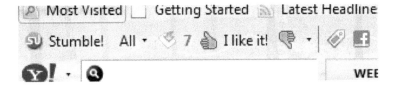

- This toolbar is one of the best toolbars I've ever seen because it allows you to quickly and easily judge a blog/website based on your general opinion. If you like the site, it gets pushed to hundreds more bloggers. If you don't like it, they take that into account as well and show it to fewer people. So with the simple click of a "Thumbs Up/Down" button, you have the power to send that blog to a hundred or more people instantly. And if they "Like It," they will send it on for you as well.

- You can add "Friends" on Stumbleupon, just like with any other social networking site, and you can actually request to see just your friends' approved sites.

- You can also request to only see articles in Facebook or Wikipedia.

- Finally, you can link your Stumbleupon account (and toolbar) with your email account to easily email pages you like and enjoy to anyone,

By E.T. Barton

whether they're your Stumbleupon friend or not. That's a very handy way to share information.

So while you may or may not convert people from looky-lous to regular-readers, the more hits your site receives, the more you go up in the Search Engine rankings, and the more visitors the Search Engines will send you. Therefore, this site is worth using (and the toolbar worth having) if for no other reason than it might make your site go "viral" (i.e., out to thousands and hundreds of thousands of people very quickly).

Word of Caution: Again, this site does not like solely self-promotion...they will block you if they realize you are only promoting yourself. Therefore, you will want to occasionally hit the Like Button for other articles and blogs you're on, as well as hitting the "Stumble" button to see what else they have to offer.

By E.T. Barton

Other Social Networking Sites

There are many other sites you can join to promote your work – and Ping will easily share your blog with all those social networking sites. The biggest issue, however, is the set-up time and the time it takes to find friends on those sites. You can do it yourself, or you can hire someone else to do it for you (like on Elance – a perfect task for that site). My recommendation, however, is to focus your time on Facebook, LinkedIn, Twitter, and Stumbleupon and let someone else do all the work for you on other sites. For now, here is a quick rundown of what I know about the various social networking sites.

- **YouTube:** I'm not very familiar with YouTube, but I know a LOT of bloggers get hundreds of thousands of hits directed to them from YouTube. They create video content and place it on YouTube, then direct people to their blog from their YouTube profile pages. Therefore, if you have any ideas for videos, especially videos

By E.T. Barton

that you want to share for free, post them on YouTube and then share them on your blog.

- **Digg:** The blogs that do the best on this site are the "Photo" blogs (blogs with lots of crazy/beautiful pictures) the "Slam" blogs (blogs that slam celebrities, politicians, etc), or the truly "Off the wall" type of blogs.

- **Reddit:** More cussing is allowed at this site, so anything rude, abrasive, crazy or fun does well at this site.

- **Yahoo! News Feed or Yahoo! Buzz**: Shares with people in your Yahoo! Answers community, as well as with anyone who is in your email list that has a Yahoo! account. It's a great link to share on because it's subtle in the way it shares. It also shares it with anyone searching on Yahoo!

Others I've used, but haven't seen any huge results with:

- MySpace (is kind of on its way out, but a lot of editors will still tell you that you should have an account, and you should have at least 2,500 friends).

- Google Buzz
- Delicious
- FriendFeed

LESSON # 16: Paying for Traffic

I know a lot of you won't want to read this section because you're on a budget, and you don't want to have to spend any money.   But it would be irresponsible of me not to at least tell you how to get traffic by paying for it. However, I'm going to keep this lesson short, because I don't want to waste a lot of time on information you aren't interested in.

I will say this though...if you need a jumpstart to your traffic, you may want to pay for it. The more traffic

By E.T. Barton

you get in any month, the sooner you will start getting regulars from the Search Engines.

Facebook Ads

One of the best ways for super-cheap advertising is to use Facebook Ads. With Facebook ads, you can create an ad and make a budget of $20 a day. Then, you can say how much you want to pay for each "Click" on your ad. That means, **you don't pay unless someone clicks on your ad.** This can be a huge timesaver because Facebook will show your ad to thousands and even hundreds of thousands of people, and as long as few people click on the ad, you don't pay for all that publicity.

Therefore, if you use Facebook ads, consider it your way of "Campaigning." You're getting your name (and your blog or book's name) in front of many people as possible so that they remember the name later, even if they aren't sure why.

By E.T. Barton

Quickie Rules:

- If you do advertise with Facebook, start with a $10 or $20 a day limit. It's very rare that you will actually hit that.

- Make your Pay-Per-Click bid around $0.50 a click. While that may seem a lot to pay, you probably won't get a whole lot of clicks right off the bat, but it is high enough for Facebook to take you seriously and push your ad. If you don't get a whole lot of page views, raise it $0.10 a click until you get the clicks you want.

- Make sure to be specific in who you Target as your demographic. If your blog talks about cop shows, target people who like cop shows. If your blog is aimed at women over 40, you can specify that you only want women over 40 to see your ad. The more specific you are, the more your ad will be placed in front of people who can actually covert to fans.

By E.T. Barton

- Be sure to set a limit, where you want to stop in case you do actually get a lot of clicks. You don't want to spend more than you intended.

Stumbleupon Ads

Since Stumbleupon is a good way to make your blog posts go viral, then you should consider advertising with them as well. They charge a flat rate of $0.05 per click, which means for $20 a day, you can get 400 people a day sent to your site. If those people like your blog, they will give it a thumbs up, and that 400 can turn into 4,000. It's a good way to get your blog sent out to a lot of people for a small amount of money, and they are basically guaranteeing that people will be on your site for that $0.05 per click.

<u>Quickie Rules:</u>

- You have to select a blog post that Stumbleupon will approve of first. Choose a page, and then a category that you think your blog will be successful in.

- Basically – be smart if you're going to do this. Only advertise the blog posts that have already shown some popularity with your regular readers (meaning that have gotten a lot of hits or a lot of comments). Don't advertise the blog posts that aren't doing well just because you want that blog post to become popular. It isn't popular for a reason, so don't waste your money.

Google Adwords

This is another great low-cost way to advertise. Basically, you get three lines, and some keyword terms to advertise your blog. Each keyword term has a fixed fee. Too low a Pay-per-click fee, and your ad will go nowhere. Too high, and you will end up spending all of your advertising money right away. The key here is to "Test" various ads at the same time and see which ones do the best. Then throw your money behind those ads.

Of course, there a lot of other places where you can advertise, but these three places are great places for those people who are on a budget looking to get their book/blog name in front of a lot of people fast.   The point here is to get them to your blog, and then get them to convert to subscribers.

The next chapter is about doing that final step.

LESSON # 17: Getting Subscribers

In Lesson 8, I spoke about setting up your Email Subscription list and all the important factors you need to have when you set up that email list. This lead generation system is very important. When done right, it will help you capture dozens and even hundreds of subscribers a month without you having to do anything other than set it up. It can prompt people to sign up before they leave your page. And most importantly, it can be set up to sell your book, or even nudge people into joining your email subscription list, which will allow you to promote your books and other products later on – thus making you money.

I recommended Aweber, and I'm going to recommend it again because – quite frankly – a lot can go wrong if you don't have it. Without Aweber, here's what can go wrong:

1. **You End Up Spamming Your Readers:** While yes, MailChimp is a FREE email capture account, there is one major flaw with MailChimp that I do not know how to get around. Basically, <u>they email your newest blog post EVERY TIME you post a blog</u>. That means, if you blog five times a week, your readers will get five emails from you a week. If you want to send a "Special" email advertising your newest book release, then that will make six emails they get from you that week. That means your readers will either

    a. Become desensitized to all your emails and stop opening them, or

    b. They'll unsubscribe.

By E.T. Barton

>   i. Both are major reasons for not using MailChimp.

2. **Your Email Subscription Company May Do Mass Mailings:** If this happens, then that company will be marked as Spam automatically by the email companies (like Yahoo and Google). If these email companies mark you as Spam, your readers will never get your emails, and the number of people that open your emails can drop to less than 50%. Why have an Email Subscription company if your emails aren't going to get through to everyone on your list?

3. **No Popups:** If your email subscription company has no Popup feature, you can lose as much as 30% of potential subscribers. If you get 100 subscribers a month, then that's an additional 30 people a month (and 360 people a year) that could be added to your email list, but won't because they didn't see the option while on your site. Why lose those people? Make sure you can add a Popup.

By E.T. Barton

Those are the three basic things I want you to focus on when looking for any email subscription company. I recommend Aweber because I know they've fixed these problems before they became problems.

How to Get People to Subscribe to Your Email List

While I was at the conference, I went to a promotion class and heard an editor, agent and NYT author speak. They said that writers should do contests on their site in order to capture new readers. A very intelligent writer somewhere in the middle of the room said, "But then how do we keep the same people from signing up over and over again for every new contest you do?"

"You can't," the editor said. "There are people who will sign up over and over again just because they want to win. You just have to weed them out of your subscription list."

That's too much work...and I don't want to do a lot of work. Do you?

So instead of having contests to get subscribers, YOU are going to do something else and save yourself the headache of having the same people subscribe over and over again just because they're "Contest Sluts." (We all know the term...we have several contest sluts here, I'm sure.)

What you're going to do instead of contests is to give something away for free in exchange for signing up on your email list. That something is going to be a Digital product so that you never have to do anything other than create that product.

Here are some ideas to get your started (and this is in order of importance):

Your Own Work

1. **Create a free PDF'd eBook to give away.** This eBook could teach more on whatever theme your blog is talking about, but I would recommend that you figure out the "Problem" that your

readers keep asking about, and write about that. It doesn't have to be a long PDF – it can be 10 to 40 double-spaced pages – but the point is to give something away for free that will also give people a taste of your writer's voice. (Yes, they will get a taste from your blog, but that's a blogger's voice. We all know we "talk" differently when writing a book...use your novelist's voice.)

2. **Write a mini-story on side characters from one of your series and put that in a PDF.** Think about any series you're writing. Are there any charming characters that you wanted to develop but couldn't because it would make that story too long? Or maybe the story wasn't long enough for its own book? That's where a mini-story can come in handy. You can develop those characters, and give your readers a taste of your series, without actually having to write a whole long book.

3. **Post a Cut Scene from Your Book.** You know you have one...that scene that your editor wants

cut, but you LOVE. Post it. Put it on your blog and market it as the "Before" or "After" scene that you just had to share. If your readers haven't read your book, they'll be clamoring for it afterward. And if they have read your book, they'll appreciate the trip back into your story.

4. **An Excerpt.** (Yes, I put this way down here at # 4.) While it may be tempting to just slap an excerpt from your book onto your site and give that away for free, I think it's far better to give away something that your readers might not have read already. Yes, putting an excerpt on your blog will make people want to buy your book if they haven't already...but it's no incentive for those who already own that book. Additionally, when your next book comes out, you'll get the same people trying to subscribe to read the excerpt you replace it with. Instead, I believe it's a better idea to put something fresh and new – that they don't have to pay for – so that you won't have to keep changing it with every book

that comes out. Only post an excerpt if you have nothing better to post at the time.

5. **A Video / Podcast / or Other Digital Product.** Remember, if you create any kind of videos, post them on YouTube so that people will come from that site to yours.

6. **And finally – contests – although I wouldn't recommend it.** In all honesty, with contests, you spend your money to give something away (or you give your book away) while you also get the same people subscribing-to-enter again and again. Then, you have to weed out the repeat subscribers...it's a pain.

The biggest point of promoting your own work for free is that you want your readers to get to know BOTH of your voices – your Blogger's voice AND your Novelist's voice – because there is a difference. I can't tell you how many times I've LOVED a blogger's blog, but then been horribly disappointed in their book...or vice versa...I've LOVED a novelist's books, but was disappointed in their blog. This is your chance to shine –

both in your blog and in your book. Give them something to love, even if it's only 10 pages long. Make it sing with who YOU are and who your characters are (if you can). If they love the freebie YOU created and gave away, they will *run out the door* to buy your books (or at least buy it through your website right then).

If you can't think of anything at all to create and give away, THEN give away someone else's work. Here are some more ideas.

Someone Else's Work

1. **Someone Else's Digital Freebie.** Don't have something to post right now, or you can't think of anything to post at all? You can always hit up someone you know and ask if it would be alright to share their work. For example:

2. **Ask Your Publisher:** A lot of Publishing Companies are now giving away free eBooks on their sites in order to promote the newest authors and give people a taste of their published authors'

works. Why not ask your editor if you can share the link to that information on your blog as well. (I'm sure they'll say yes, because you're marketing them for free.) Then, all you would do is post on your site that your readers can get access to free Romance eBooks every month from your publisher if they subscribe to your email. Then, when they subscribe, simply redirect the "Thank You" page at your email subscription company to the page at your Publisher's website where the free books are displayed. By doing this, you also have something to promote to your list every month when the books are changed out.

3. **Ask an Author Friend or Colleague:** Anyone that writes on your topic, and who gives their product away, may or may not be alright with letting you share their information. After all, you are marketing their product for free as well.

4. **Project Gutenberg Site (www.Gutenberg.org):** This site is another good site to use to promote free eBooks. Say you're blogging about Sir

By E.T. Barton

Arthur Conan Doyle's book for the next month. You can offer the "Sherlock Holmes" eBook for free to your readers – in exchange for signing up for you list – and then direct them to the link that actually allows them to download it for free legally. This site has thousands of free eBooks and allows anyone to download the information directly to their computers.

5. **And of course, any videos or digital files that someone else is giving away for free and wouldn't mind you sharing.**

Once you have a product in mind that you want to post, create a Landing Page for it. Advertise the product as if you were selling it, and include pictures, testimonials, quotes, etc., to encourage people to subscribe. Next, upload the digital file to your "Media" section in your blog. After the product is uploaded, you will be given an URL for that file. Go to your email subscription company and enter the Media URL from your blog as the webpage to direct your readers too once they have finished the subscription process. By doing

By E.T. Barton

so, your readers will be able to download the product themselves and you will never have to do anything again.

YOUR ASSIGNMENT:

Create or Find a Digital Product that you can link to your Subscriber list. Since this is pretty important for building your subscriber list, you want to get started on something right away. Post something from your book, if you have something available, or just make something up quickly that your readers might want to share.

<u>The key here is – if people aren't subscribing to get your free digital product, you may not be marketing it well enough (or making it sound interesting enough), and you should consider switching your product for something new, or recreating your landing page so your freebie sounds bad-ass.</u>

LESSON # 18: Comments, Guest Blogging, and Links – Oh My!

At this point in the lesson plan – nearing the end, that is – you should now be blogging in a way that's attractive to your readers and the Search Engines. You should also be using keywords and plug-ins, pictures and social networking sites... you should be blogging more like a money-making blogger and less like someone writing a diary.

You should be solving a problem related to a very specific niche that you are an expert at.

By E.T. Barton

Hopefully, you should also be making some money with Google Adsense, and your traffic numbers should be higher. Now, let's drive them a *lot* higher.

To do that, there are three things you should focus on: Comments, Guest Blogging and Links. Each topic can bring in more traffic, and there are two sides to each topic. Here's a fast, concentrated rundown on each.

Getting Comments

A lot of people are asking me, "How do I get comments on my blog? What do I need to do?"

Comments are a tricky business to get. Sometimes you get a lot on a blog you didn't really like, and sometimes you get NONE on a blog you thought kicked butt. Be aware that not every blog you post will get comments. Some of your regulars will do so out of respect, but most won't have time. You have to really suck your readers into your posts by putting forth your best work and blowing their mind.

By E.T. Barton

Here's what you need to focus your articles on to make that happen...(I'm going to use personal stories from my blogs because I'm not sure how better to make the examples relate...so sorry in advance for the cheap self-promotion.)

1. **Tell a Personal Story:** People respond to stories – they love them. They want to see what you're talking about in their heads, and your skills as a romance writer can really come in handy. But the key here is not so much about "just telling a story" as it is about being personal. Tell people the things you might hold back because you think it makes you look silly or foolish. Pretend like your readers are your best girlfriend and share with them the problems you've had and conquered. You don't have to go into vivid detail, but you can generalize. The more you reveal stories about your life, the more people will be able to relate to you, and the more they will ask you for more information.

By E.T. Barton

a. Example: One of the blogs on my Bookkeeping blog that really seemed to hit home with a lot of people was the post I wrote about quitting a terrible, terrible job. I spoke about how awful my boss treated me, and the final straw that made me decide to never work for anyone else again. A LOT of bookkeepers responded. It was a problem they could relate to, and it resulted in a lot of emails asking for personal advice.

2. **Be Controversial:** The more controversial any blog post you write is, the more comments you'll get from your readers. In fact, not only will you get comments, you will actually get arguments from readers. Then those arguments will be rebutted by other readers who agree with what you're saying. So if you're writing about a touchy subject, take a stand and be controversial. Sure, you may piss some readers off, but controversy does result in comments, and it gives you a chance to really get to know your readers.

By E.T. Barton

a. Example: One of the most controversial blogs I ever wrote was called "How to Bully a Debt Collector." That one article caused such a landslide of positive and negative comments, I felt overwhelmed. In fact, I nearly removed the blog post because I couldn't handle some of the terrible things some debt collectors were saying about me and my advice. The point of that article was to empower people that needed advice on dealing with their debt, but debt collectors interpreted it as an attack on debt collectors in general, and a crusade for people to blow their debt off. Finally, I had to stop reading the comments because they would just bug me for days. That is definitely one thing you can expect with controversial blogs.

3. **Solve a Problem:** This part is like what your teachers always told you in school: "For every question you want to ask about a problem,

someone else wants to ask the same question, but doesn't because they're afraid. You can ask that question for them, and then that other person gets their answer as well."   This applies to your blog because as you set yourself apart as an expert, you'll find your readers will begin to ask your advice.   When they ask your advice, they're bringing a personal problem to your attention that you can solve or help them find an answer for. Make the problem anonymous, and then write about it on your blog. You'd be amazed at how many people will thank you for that, because they wanted the information, but they didn't want to bother you.

   a. Example: The most popular series on my blog is the "Diary of a Bad, Bad Bookkeeper" series. Why – because it brings up common small business embezzlement issues that most business owners don't even know to ask about. They may think they're bookkeeper is embezzling, but they can't be certain.

They don't know what to look for, and I answer that before they even ask. Every time I post a blog, I get comments on all of my social media sites.

4. **Teach Something Your Readers Really Want to Know:** Your readers are reading your blog for a reason. Maybe that reason is because they like you; maybe it's because they like what you're writing about. Either way, you have an opportunity to share your knowledge with them in a unique way, and to teach them something that may be common knowledge to you, but will rock their world. So be the teacher while you have their ear, and teach something that they really want to know about.

   a. Example: On my Babies and Baggage blog, one of the first blogs I posted was called "Family Travel Deals: Cheap Airfare from LAX to Sydney." In that blog, I proceeded to tell people how I found roundtrip airfare from Los Angeles to Sydney for less than $400 (before taxes), step-by-step. Within the first week, I had over 125 comments, which was a shocking record for me. At the last count, I had over 200 comments on that blog. Why? Because people really want to know how to find cheap airfare, and I taught them how to do it. Simple concept – lots of gratitude.

5. **Finally, Share Information They Just Can't Find Anywhere Else:** There are things people want information to that they just can't seem to find. If you know where to find it, share it. Make landing pages that advertise that information. Create links to it. Write posts about it. Not only will it set you apart as an expert, but it will also fill a need your readers have.

   a. Example: On my blog, Airlines That Fly To, all I do is create list blogs that tell what airlines fly to what countries and cities. People have been looking for that information for so long, they leave tons of comments thanking me for the information. They even tell me that they bookmark my site and forward it to family and friends. <u>But all it is a database of information.</u> That's what people want – information. Give it to them.

To find topics to talk about that people want to know about...the key is keywords. Do your searches and find what people really want to know about. Then, get personal, teach something, share info, and new people will start commenting all the time. Just don't be offended if those comments are negative, because even negative comments create links back to your site, and help make your site more popular.

Giving Comments

Believe it or not, commenting on other peoples' blogs can also bring you traffic. When you leave a comment, you create a link from that site to your site. People can follow that link back to your blog. The key, however, is not to leave *stupid* comments, but intelligent and thoughtful comments. The more thoughtful or informative your comment, the more people will wonder about you and what you know. So, to give comments that bring traffic, visit the "Big Boys" in your field (those bloggers in your niche who are dominating the market), and start leaving comments on multiple blogs. The more comments you leave, the more that blogger's readers will become familiar with your name, and the more they'll pop over to check out your site as well.

The other bonus: That blogger will get to know you as well, and in the future, you may be able to approach them about networking together. The more powerful bloggers you have in your network, the faster your blog will grow.

One more thing to remember: **All comments, whether good, bad or ugly, can help your blog get traffic (except for Spam).** So don't be offended if someone leaves a negative comment. Simply post a neutral or friendly reply to rebut their argument, and leave it on for the link they've created. The only comments you really will want to delete, are the ones

By E.T. Barton

that are obviously spam. While you may be tempted to leave those – because they do create a link as well – the sad truth is that many spammers now are leading people to sites with viruses. Delete any comments that are blatantly self promotional, because those kind of comments can hurt your readers instead of protect them.

Linking Up

As your blog becomes popular, people will begin to approach you about "Linking Up" with their site. Some of those people will only be interested in getting your traffic to go to their site, while others will be genuinely interested in creating an alliance. It's up to you to decide which sites you want to link to and which ones you don't.

There are three ways I know of to link up to someone's site.

1. You can add their website url to your blogroll, and then display your blogroll in your Sidebar.
2. You can add their url to a special page on your blog that leads people from their site to yours.
3. You can create a picture ad that links to their site.

Then they would take your website url and do one or more of these items on their site.

The key here is that you can technically make money on any of these items, or even use these items to get other people to promote your blog.

A writer in LARA used this tool very effectively. She would offer people two choices in linking up with her rapidly-growing blog. They could "advertise their books on her blog" for $25, which would then have the books on her home page for one to three months. OR, someone could have a book advertisement on her blog for free, but only in exchange for putting a BIG Banner Advertisement about her book on their blog (in a prominent position) for free. As you can imagine, it resulted in her book being promoted on a lot of writer's blogs in exchange for a posting about that writer's book. It was a very successful quid-pro-quo that other writers soon began to recommend to new writers for promotional purposes.

Thus, the two sides of linking are, you put a link on your site to someone else's, and they put a link on their site to yours.

Other Lesson Learned:

Linking up is not only a great way to promote your book and build a strong network, it is also a fantastic way for you to make a <u>monthly income</u> for advertising other people's blogs, books and digital products on your site.

Guest Blogging

The two sides to guest blogging are having people blog on your site (which can help you fill your minimum weekly blogging requirements), and blogging on other people's sites. Both ways are excellent sources of traffic.

Consider this: You ask someone to be a guest blogger and they write up an interesting post for you. Not only do you advertise this blog to your social networking sites, but they also advertise your blog to THEIR social networking sites because they want everyone they know to be aware of their "accomplishment." (After all, to many writers, being published *anywhere* can feel like an accomplishment.) If that writer has 1,000 regular fans, those fans are going to pop over to see proof of the accomplishment. Boom – instant traffic.

The key here is to allow the guest blogger to post a portion of their blog on their site, but then to cut it off part way down and create a link to your site at the end. By doing so, they will be led to your site, and it creates a link between both of your websites (good for both of you). Also, you will want to add a link at the top or bottom of the post that leads to the other blogger's site. Again, Linking Up leads to traffic.

By E.T. Barton

The Flip Side: You do a blog for someone, which makes you look even more like an expert in your field. You get to link your guest blog post to your site, which leads the readers from that site to yours. The key here is to try to get your blog posts put on sites that are more popular than yours. You can do this by randomly sending them guest posts and hoping they'll publish one, or just emailing them and asking them if they're interested in what you have to say. (Most bloggers will be only too happy to post someone else's work and *not* claim it as their own because it widens the horizons of their blog.) There's no harm in trying, and so many benefits to gain.

And there you have it...eighteen ways to improve your blog and start making money from it.

www.ingramcontent.com/pod-product-compliance
Lightning Source LLC
Chambersburg PA
CBHW071544080326
40689CB00061B/1821